Academic Writing and Pub

Do you struggle with submission notes and grapple with guidelines for authors?

This lively and readable guide will be invaluable for postgraduates, lecturers and researchers new to academic writing and publishing.

James Hartley calls upon his wealth of knowledge accrued over many years to help seasoned writers too, with practical suggestions based on up-to-date research.

Academic Writing and Publishing guides the reader through the process of writing and publishing. Packed with examples and evaluations of recent work, the book is presented in short chapters to reflect the writing and publishing process. Written in a lively and personal style, the advice is direct and practical. Divided into four parts, this accessible text:

- discusses the nature of academic writing and examines how different individuals tackle the task;
- dissects the journal article and outlines research findings on how to write its constituent parts;
- examines other types of academic writing: books, theses, conference papers, letters to the editor etc.;
- describes other aspects of academic writing – dealing with publishing delays, procrastination and collaborating with others.

James Hartley is Research Professor at the School of Psychology, The University of Keele, UK.

Academic Writing and Publishing

A practical handbook

James Hartley

Routledge
Taylor & Francis Group

LONDON AND NEW YORK

First published 2008
by Routledge
2 Park Square, Milton Park, Abingdon, Oxon OX14 4RN

Simultaneously published in the USA and Canada
by Routledge
270 Madison Ave, New York, NY 10016

Routledge is an imprint of the Taylor & Francis Group, an informa business

© 2008 James Hartley

Typeset in Garamond 3 and Gill Sans by
Florence Production Ltd, Stoodleigh, Devon
Printed and bound in Great Britain by
TJ International Ltd, Padstow, Cornwall

British Library Cataloguing in Publication Data
A catalogue record for this book is available from the British Library

Library of Congress Cataloging in Publication Data
Hartley, James, 1940–
     Academic writing and publishing : a practical guide / James Hartley.
          p. cm.
          Includes bibliographical references and index.
     1. Authorship.   2. Academic writing.   3. Scholarly publishing.
     I. Title.
     PN146.H373 2008
     808′.02 – dc22   2007044058

ISBN10: 0–415–45321–6 (hbk)
ISBN10: 0–415–45322–4 (pbk)
ISBN10: 0–203–92798–2 (ebk)

ISBN13: 978–0–415–45321–9 (hbk)
ISBN13: 978–0–415–45322–6 (pbk)
ISBN13: 978–0–203–92798–4 (ebk)

Contents

Tables and figures

Figures

Tables

Acknowledgements

Many colleagues have helped – directly and indirectly – with the publication of this text, and I am indebted to them all.

Much of the material has been reworked from previous journal articles. I am grateful to Baywood Publications (Chapters 2.1 and 4.7), Sage Publications (Chapter 2.4), the British Psychological Society (Chapters 2.12 and 4.4), Elsevier (Chapter 3.7) and Tyrell Burgess Associates (Chapter 4.5) for permission to re-present these ideas.

I am also indebted to Richard Slatcher and James Pennebaker for permission to use examples from an article of theirs to illustrate points made in Chapters 2.4 through to 2.7, and to John Coleman and Andrew Knipe for technical assistance.

Section 1

Introduction

The nature of academic writing

> Anyone who wishes to become a good writer should endeavour, before he allows himself to be tempted by the more showy qualities, to be direct, simple, brief, vigorous, and lucid.
>
> (Fowler & Fowler, 1906, p. 11)

THE LANGUAGE OF SCIENCE AND ACADEMIA

If we examine the text of scientific articles it is clear that there is a generally accepted way of writing them. Scientific text is precise, impersonal and objective. It typically uses the third person, the passive tense, complex terminology, and various footnoting and referencing systems.

Such matters are important when it comes to learning how to write scientific articles. Consider, for example, the following advice:

> Good scientific writing is characterised by objectivity. This means that a paper must present a balanced discussion of a range of views . . . Moreover, value judgements, which involve moral beliefs of what is 'right' or 'wrong' must be avoided . . . The use of personal pronouns is unnecessary, and can lead to biases or unsupported assumptions. In scientific papers, therefore, personal pronouns should not be used. When you write a paper, unless you attribute an opinion to someone else, it is understood to be your own. Phrases such as 'in my opinion' or 'I think,' therefore, are superfluous and a waste of words . . . For the same reasons, the plural pronouns *we* and *our* are not used.
>
> (Cited, with permission, from Smyth, 1996, pp. 2–3)

CLARITY IN SCIENTIFIC WRITING

In my view, following this sort of advice obscures rather than clarifies the text. Indeed, Smyth has rather softened his views with the passage of time (see Smyth, 2004). For me, the views expressed by Fowler and Fowler in 1906, which head this chapter, seem more appropriate. Consider, for example, the following piece by Watson and Crick, announcing their discovery of the structure of DNA, written in 1953. Note how this text contravenes almost all of Smyth's strictures cited above:

> We wish to suggest a structure for the salt of deoxyribose nucleic acids (D.N.A.). This structure has novel features which are of considerable biological interest.
>
> A structure for nucleic acid has already been proposed by Pauling and Corey. They kindly made their manuscript available to us in advance of publication. Their model consists of three inter-twined chains, with the phosphates near the fibre axis, and the bases on the outside. In our opinion this structure is unsatisfactory for two reasons: (1) We believe that the material which gives the X-ray diagrams is the salt, not the free acid. Without the acidic hydrogen atoms it is not clear what forces would hold the structure together, especially as the negatively charged phosphates near the axis will repel each other. (2) Some of the van der Waals distances appear too small.
>
> Another three-chain structure has also been suggested by Fraser (in the press). In his model the phosphates are on the outside and the bases on the inside, linked together by hydrogen bonds. This structure as described is rather ill-defined, and for this reason we shall not comment on it.
>
> (Opening paragraphs from Watson and Crick, 1953, pp. 737–8, reproduced with permission from James D. Watson and Macmillan Publishers Ltd)

Table 1.1.1 lists some of the comments that different people have made about academic text. Some consider that academic writing is spare, dull and undistinguished. Some consider that articles in prestigious journals will be more difficult to read than articles in less-respected journals ones because of

Table 1.1.1 Some characteristics of academic writing

Academic writing is:
- unnecessarily complicated
- pompous, long-winded, technical
- impersonal, authoritative, humourless
- elitist, and excludes outsiders.

But it can be:
- appropriate in specific circumstances
- easier for non-native speakers to follow.

their greater use of technical vocabulary. Others warn against disguising poor-quality articles in an eloquent style. Indeed, there is some evidence that journals do become less readable as they become more prestigious and that academics and students do judge complex writing to be more erudite than simpler text (Hartley *et al.*, 1988; Oppenheimer, 2005; Shelley and Schuh, 2001). Furthermore, Sokal (1996) once famously wrote a spoof article in scientific and sociological jargon that went undetected by the editors (and presumably the referees) of the journal it was submitted to.

MEASURING THE DIFFICULTY OF ACADEMIC TEXT

There are many different ways of measuring the difficulty of academic text. Three different kinds of measure (which can be used in combination) are: 'expert-based', 'reader-based' and 'text-based', respectively (Schriver, 1989).

- *Expert-based* methods are ones that use experts to make assessments of the effectiveness of a piece of text. Referees, for example, are typically asked to judge the quality of an article submitted for publication in a scientific journal, and they frequently make comments about the clarity of the writing. Similarly, subject-matter experts are asked by publishers to judge the suitability of a manuscript submitted for publication in terms of content and difficulty.
- *Reader-based* methods are ones that involve the actual readers in making assessments of the text. Readers might be asked to complete evaluation scales, to state their preferences for different versions of the same texts, to comment on sections of text that they find difficult to follow, or be tested on how much they can recall after reading a text.
- *Text-based* measures are ones that can be used without recourse to experts or to readers, and these focus on the text itself. Such measures include computer-based readability formulae and computer-based measures of style and word use.

Two particular measures deserve attention here because they have both been used to assess the readability of academic text. One is a reader-based measure, called the 'cloze' test. The other is a computer-based measure, called the Flesch 'Reading Ease' score.

Cloze tests

The cloze test was originally developed in 1953 to measure people's understanding of text. Here, samples from a passage are presented to readers with, say, every sixth word missing. The readers are then required to fill in the missing words.

Technically speaking, if every sixth word is deleted, then six versions should be prepared, with the gaps each starting from a different point. However, it is more common _____ prepare one version and perhaps _____ to focus the gaps on _____ words. Whatever the procedure, the _____ are scored either:

(a) by _____ accepting as correct those responses _____ directly match what the original _____ actually said, or
(b) by _____ these together with acceptable synonyms.

As the two scoring methods (a) and (b) correlate highly, it is more objective to use the tougher measure of matching exact words (in this case: 'to', 'even', 'important', 'passages', 'only', 'which' 'author' and 'accepting').

Test scores can be improved by having the gaps more widely dispersed (say every tenth word); by varying the lengths of the gaps to match the lengths of the missing words; by providing the first of the missing letters; by having a selection of words to choose from for each gap; or by having readers work in pairs or small groups. These minor variations, however, do not affect the main purpose of the cloze procedure, which is to assess readers' comprehension of the text and, by inference, its difficulty.

The cloze test can be used by readers both concurrently and retrospectively. It can be presented concurrently (as in the paragraph above) as a test of comprehension, and readers are required to complete it, or it can be presented retrospectively, and readers are asked to complete it after they have first read the original text. In this case the test can serve as a measure of recall as well as comprehension. The cloze test can also be used to assess the effects on readers' comprehension of different textual organisations, readers' prior knowledge and other textual features, such as illustrations, tables and graphs (Reid *et al.*, 1983).

There are few studies using the cloze test with academic text. However, it has been used (along with other measures) to assess the readability of original and revised versions of journal abstracts (Hartley, 1994).

The Flesch Reading Ease score

The Flesch score is (now) one of many easily obtained computer-based measures of text readability. The scores run from 0 to 100, and the higher the score, the easier the text. The original measure was created in 1943 by Rudolph Flesch to measure the readability of magazine articles (Klare, 1963). Basically, what current measures of the score do is to count the length of the words and the length of the sentences in a passage and compute these into a reading ease (RE) score (Flesch, 1948). The underlying logic is clear – the longer the sentences, and the longer the words within them, the more difficult the text will be. Scores can be grouped into the categories shown in Table 1.1.2.

Table 1.1.2 Flesch scores and their interpretation

Flesch RE score	Reading age	Difficulty level	Example for UK readers
90–100	10–11 years	Very easy	Children's stories
80–89	11–12 years	Easy	Women's fiction
70–79	12–13 years	Fairly easy	Popular novels
60–69	14–15 years	Average	Tabloid newspapers
50–59	16–17 years	Fairly difficult	Introductory textbooks
30–49	18–20 years	Difficult	Students' essays
0–29	Graduate	Very difficult	Academic articles

Adapted from Hartley, Sotto and Fox (2004), p. 193. © Sage Publications.

Academic text typically falls into the 'difficult' and the 'very difficult' categories.

There are a number of obvious limitations to this measure (along with most other computer-based measures of readability). The formula was developed in the 1940s for use with popular reading materials rather than academic text: it is thus somewhat dated and not entirely appropriate in the current context. The notion that the longer the words and the longer the sentences, then the more difficult the text, although generally true, is naïve. Some short sentences are very difficult to understand. Thus the calculations do not take into account the meaning of the text to the reader (and you will get the same score if you process the text backwards), nor do they take into account the readers' prior knowledge about the topic in question, or their motivation – both essential contributions to reading difficulty.

Nonetheless, despite these limitations, the Flesch score has been widely used to assess the readability of academic text, partly because it is a convenient tool on most writers' personal computers. It is simple and easy to run and keeps a check on the difficulty level of what you are writing as you proceed. It is also useful as a measure of the relative difficulty of two or more versions of the same text – we might well agree that one version with a Flesch score of 50 is likely to be easier to read than another version with a score of 30, and that some useful information might be obtained if we use the scores to make comparisons between different texts, and between different versions of the same text.

Some examples might serve to illustrate this. My colleagues and I, for instance, once carried out four separate studies using the Flesch and other computer-based measures of text to test the idea that influential articles would in fact be more readable than would be less influential ones (Hartley *et al.*, 2002). In the first two of these studies, we compared the readability of sections from famous articles in psychology with that of sections from the articles that immediately followed them in the same journals (and were not famous). In the second two studies, we compared the readability of highly cited articles in psychology with that of similar controls. The results showed that the famous articles were significantly easier to read than were their controls (average Flesh scores of 33 versus 25), but that this did not occur for the highly cited articles (average Flesch scores of 26 and 25).

In another study, we compared the readability of texts in the sciences, the arts and the social sciences, written in various genres (Hartley *et al.*, 2004). Here, we compared extracts in all three disciplines from sets of research articles, text-books for colleagues, text-books for students, specialist magazine articles and magazine articles for the general public. The main finding here was not surprising – the texts got easier to read as measured by the Flesch scores as they moved across the genres, from 15 to 60. There was little support, however, for our notion that the scientific texts would be easier to read than those in the other disciplines *within* each of the different genres.

In a third example, we used Flesch scores, together with data from other computer-based measures, to examine the relative readability of the abstracts, introductions, and discussions from eighty academic papers in psychology (Hartley *et al.*, 2003). Here the abstracts scored lowest in terms of readability (mean score of 18), the introductions came next (mean score of 21), and the discussions did best of all (mean score 23). Intriguingly, although the mean scores of the different sections differed, the authors wrote in stylistically consistent ways across the sections. Thus, readability was variable across the sections, but consistent within the authors.

THE STRUCTURE OF SCIENTIFIC ARTICLES

Research articles typically have a standard structure to facilitate communication, which is known as IMRAD (introduction, method, results and discussion), although, of course, there are variations on this basic format. The chapters that follow in Section 2 of this book elaborate on each IMRAD section in more detail. It is important to note here, of course, that this structure is actually a charade. Scientists do not proceed in the way that IMRAD implies. IMRAD is a formula for writing up, and it is a method for making the scientific enterprise look much more logical than it actually is (see Medawar, 1964). Similarly, although the language of the scientific article may appear to be precise, impersonal and objective (as noted at the beginning of this chapter), this, too, is misleading. The language of scientific text is also the language of rhetoric and persuasion. Table 1.1.3 lists some rhetorical devices that the reader will no doubt find in this text!

WRITING PROCESSES

The discussion so far has concentrated on the *product* of writing – the academic paper and its constituents – rather than the *process* – how academics go about

Table 1.1.3 Some rhetorical devices used in academic articles to persuade the reader of the validity of the argument

Jargon: language that can become pretentious and opaque.

Misuse of references: lists of references to support a point, and selective references to support one side of the argument and not the other.

Straw men arguments: to bolster a position.

Vague qualifiers: e.g. 'Most people will agree ...' – to ensure the reader does or does not, as appropriate.

Quotations: selectively used to support a point with particular emphasis.

Anecdotes: used like quotations.

Examples: the most dramatic ones selected from a range.

Exclamation marks and question marks: to speak more directly to, and carry along, the readers.

Omissions: especially in abstracts, of key details such as the numbers of participants, their ages and where the study was carried out.

Overstatements: discussing non-significant findings as though they are statistically significant.

Distortions: selective presentation of findings from previous research and in the current research.

After Woods (1999), pp. 63–80.

writing. I now want to discuss writing processes in more detail, and differences between writers in this respect.

The research on how writers actually produce texts can be considered in terms of a hierarchy of overlapping processes or levels. At the bottom level, there is the actual process of putting pen to paper or, these days, fingers to keyboard. Next comes a concern with the thinking that leads to text being written or to being keyboarded. And finally, there is discussion of writing in a more social context: how and why people write at university, for example, and how producing a publication is a lengthy business.

Level 1: Keyboarding the text

Research at this level of detail is not particularly relevant to this text. However, it is of interest in one respect. In the old days, people produced and kept early drafts of their work. It was possible, therefore, to see how – through the changes, deletions and revisions – a writer's thoughts changed and developed as the text was produced. Today, with word processing, it is extremely difficult to keep track of changes of this kind. It is now so easy to change a word or phrase without affecting the look of the manuscript, and early versions are deleted and changed online as the text develops. (Of course, some obsessive authors such as myself keep copies of initial and later versions, but it is hard to think of them as sequential, separate *drafts*, as was the case before . . .).

Nonetheless, some word processing systems do allow writers/readers to keep track of the changes made, and such changes have been subject to analysis (e.g. see Kollberg and Eklundh, 2001; Wengelin, 2007). Kollberg and Eklund, for instance, described a computer-based technique for analysing the text production and revision strategies of school-children and university students. Using keystroke analyses, these investigators were able to create a record of all the revisions made to a text while it was being written, as well as the order in which they were made. One can imagine that such records may be useful in, say, the study of literary criticism, or in relation to studies at Level 2.

Level 2: Writing and thinking

The research on how writers actually think about their texts as they produce them is typified by observational and retrospective accounts. In observational studies, it is usual to use 'protocol analysis' as a technique, where writers are asked to comment on what they are doing and thinking about as they are writing (e.g. see Cotton and Gresty, 2006). Retrospective accounts are given in response to questions after the writing session is over. Sometimes, writing sessions are videotaped to aid subsequent analysis. Interviews and questionnaires are also commonly used in retrospective studies to ask writers about their writing procedures. Table 1.1.4 shows the level of detail described in some of these studies.

Studies using these methodologies lead to the conclusion that what drives writing is very much:

(i)   who the text is being written for;
(ii) what it is about; and
(iii) how much of the text has been already produced (Hayes, 2006).

Within these constraints, writing is often characterised as a hierarchically organised, goal-directed, problem-solving process. Writing, it is said, consists of four main recursive processes – planning, writing, editing and reviewing. These activities, however, do not necessarily occur in the fixed order suggested. Writers move to and fro in accordance with their individual goals of the moment – although, naturally, more time is spent on planning or thinking at the start, and on editing and reviewing at the end.

Studies of the teaching of writing have shown that instruction in each of these activities leads to better performance (e.g. see Graham, 2006). However, some authors, such as Peter Elbow, think that it is misleading to think of

Table 1.1.4 Multiple and overlapping thought processes when writing

While I am writing, my mind is either simultaneously engaged in or rapidly switching between processes that perform all or most of the following functions:

- monitoring the thematic coherence of the text;
- searching for and retrieving relevant content;
- identifying lexical items associated with this content;
- formulating syntactic structures;
- inflecting words to give them the necessary morphology;
- monitoring for appropriate register;
- ensuring that the intended new text is tied into the immediately preceding text in a way that maintains cohesion;
- formulating and executing motor plans for key strokes that will form the text on screen;
- establishing the extent to which the just-generated clause or sentence moves the text as a whole nearer the intended goal; and
- revising goals in the light of new ideas cued by the just-produced text.

These processes cannot all be performed simultaneously. Attempting to do so ... would result in overload and writing would stop. The fact that I am writing this at all, therefore, is testament to the writing system's ability to co-ordinate and schedule a number of different processes within the limited processing resources afforded to it by my mind.

Adapted, with permission, from Torrance and Galbraith (2006), p. 67, and the Guilford Press.

writing as moving in separate stages from planning through writing and editing to reviewing. Elbow advocates writing some appropriate text first, not worrying too much at this point about spelling and syntax, and then repeatedly editing and refining the text to clarify what it is one wants to say (e.g. see Elbow, 1998). There is room, of course, for both positions. It can be helpful to think about the sequence and the structure of a paper (or book chapter) before one begins to write it, but one need not necessarily start at the beginning. And it can be equally helpful to let the thoughts pour out when writing a particular section, before revising it. In my view, the actual product determines the process, but the processes involved can be many and varied.

Individual differences in academic writing

Numerous investigators have tried to distinguish between writers in terms of the ways that they think about their writing and their procedures. As we have already seen, computer-based tools can be used to measure different aspects of style (or readability). Microsoft's *Office* program, for instance, provides measures of word, sentence and paragraph lengths, the percentage of passives used, and various measures of readability (such as the Flesch RE score). Another program, Pennebaker's *Linguistic Inquiry and Word Count*

(Pennebaker *et al.*, 2001), calculates the percentage of words used in any one text in any one of seventy-four different linguistic categories. Some of these separate categories can be grouped, for example, into emotional words (e.g. 'happy', 'sad', 'angry'), self-references (e.g. 'I', 'we') and cognitive words (e.g. 'realise', 'think', 'understand').

Studies using these measures have confirmed that individual writers have distinct styles or 'voices'. My colleagues and I, for example, once showed that three highly productive writers maintained similar writing styles over a period of more than thirty years, despite the many changes in the technology that they had used over this period (Hartley *et al.*, 2001). Indeed, 'forensic linguistics' is a discipline that specialises in detecting changes in authorship (e.g. in a witness's statement) by using computer-based stylistic measures (e.g. see Coulthard, 2004).

So, although all the articles in a particular journal may look much the same, different writers will have used different methods to achieve this uniformity. Indeed, as noted above, one of the ways that manuscripts differed, before the advent of word processing, was in their physical appearance. Stephen Spender, the poet, distinguished between writers he labelled 'Beethovians' and those who he labelled 'Mozartians', and, if you have ever seen an original (or facsimile) manuscript of either of these composers, you will know exactly what he meant. A score by Beethoven is full of crossings out and looks an incomprehensible mess. A score by Mozart is, by contrast, neat and pristine. Beethoven, it can be argued, working from earlier sketches in his notebooks, was struggling to get it right. Mozart had it right already in his head and just copied it out:

> When I proceed to write down my ideas, I take out of the bag of my memory, if I may use that phrase, what has been previously collected into it in the way that I have mentioned (above). For this reason the committing to paper is done quickly enough, for everything is, as I said before, already finished; and it rarely differs on paper from what was in my imagination.
>
> (Excerpt from a letter attributed to Mozart, in Ghiselin, 1980, p. 35)

In modern terminology it is more common to distinguish between writers who are 'pre-planners' (Mozartians) and 'revisers' (Beethovians). Indeed, several studies distinguished between academic writers in terms of these two separate categories before the advent of word processing. Others, however, placed them along a spectrum – from pre-planners to revisers. Thus, for example, Torrance *et al.* (1994) described postgraduates in the social sciences who:

(i) extensively pre-planned their writing and then made few revisions (planners);

(ii) developed their content and structure through extensive revisions (revisers); and

(iii) both planned before they started to write and revised extensively as part of their writing process (mixed).

Torrance *et al.* found that their postgraduate planners reported higher productivity than did both the revisers and the mixed groups. Table 1.1.5 provides quotations from fully fledged academics to illustrate what these different kinds of writer say. It is not necessary, of course, to stick to one particular method. John Le Carré, for example, in a radio broadcast, reported using a storyboard method for planning three of his novels but letting the plot develop for others.

Some research with adolescents suggests that writing and changing what you want to say as you go along (revising) lead to better writing than planning the writing in advance and then writing it out (planning). However, more recent research along these lines suggests that there might be further individual differences here. Kieft (2006), for instance, found in one of her studies that 15 to 16-year-old students who were *high* self-monitors – i.e. those who frequently evaluated their text as they were writing – did equally well whether or not they were taught to revise through multiple-drafting or to produce an outline first. However, those who were *low* self-monitors did better when they were taught to produce an outline first.

Other investigators have used fancier names for describing different kinds of writer. Nonetheless, they are arguing essentially the same thing – that there is a variety of writing styles based along a spectrum from pre-planning at the start to revising at the end. Thus Chandler (1995), for example, distinguished between 'architects' (planners in advance), 'oil-painters'

Table 1.1.5 Quotations from academic writers

I like to write a plan. I produce section headings and fairly detailed jottings about what these will contain, and then follow them through.

I write very much in sections at a time, from the beginning to the end.

I do plan my writing, but I usually find that in the process of writing the plan might take a new direction. I will then 'go with the flow'.

I usually pre-plan it, although on the occasions when I have just let it 'flow' it seems to have worked quite well.

Cut and paste was invented for me. I start off with headings . . . I then start shifting things around.

I have ideas in the back of my mind, but I only really know what I want to say as I write them down. That drives me into more reading and re-reading of my texts.

Reproduced from Wellington (2003), pp. 22–3, with permission of the author and the publishers.

(changers and revisers), 'bricklayers' (one step at a time) and 'water-colourists' (who aim to complete the text at the first attempt).

The architect strategy is typically the 'plan, write and revise' strategy discussed above. Architects make detailed plans and stick to them. Oil painters may think of new ideas while they are writing. They tend to produce drafts and print them out while they are working. This allows them to read and to revise. A characteristic refrain of these writers is, 'How do I know what I am going to say until I can see what I have said?'. Sharples (1999) classifies the novelists Frederick Forsyth as a water-colourist and Beryl Bainbridge as a bricklayer.

Individual differences and new technology

I am inclined these days to the view that new technology has made it more difficult to categorise and describe differences in the ways that writers go about writing. Word processors allow writers to write how they like at whim, and to vary their approaches. But writing is still a complex business, however, even with word processors. The writing strategies described above in Table 1.1.5 do not begin to approach the fine detail of what is actually required. Table 1.1.4 gives a better picture.

Level 3: Social aspects of academic writing

Academic writing does not take place in a social vacuum, and the motives for writing are mixed and various. Today's academics are expected to produce papers, and their livelihood depends upon it. This affects what is researched, who does it, who writes it up, where it is published, and so on. Figure 1.1.1 presents the reasons for writing listed by Orhan Pamuk, winner of the 2006 Nobel Prize in Literature.

Murray and Moore (2006) describe academic writing as consisting of advances and retreats. There are things that drive us on – such as creating new knowledge, and gaining approval – and there are things that hold us back – such as difficulties in getting started, revising the text, finding our voice and generally feeling inadequate. Then there are inordinate delays in the publishing process, together with referees' comments that can be quite dispiriting. Writing for publication can be thoroughly enjoyable at times, and nasty and competitive at others.

Murray and Moore discuss how things that facilitate and things that inhibit writing are moderated both by environmental factors (such as time available to write) and internal factors (such as writing fluency). Furthermore, successful writing is affected by intrinsic rewards (such as personal satisfaction) and extrinsic ones (such as promotion and tenure). Figure 1.1.2 shows how these factors interact.

As you know, the question we writers are asked most often, the favourite question, is: why do you write? I write because I have an innate need to write! I write because I can't do normal work like other people. I write because I want to read other books like the ones I write. I write because I am angry at all of you, angry at everyone. I write because I love sitting in a room all day writing. I write because I can only partake in real life by changing it. I write because I want others, all of us, the whole world to know what sort of life we lived, and continue to live, in Istanbul, in Turkey. I write because I love the smell of paper, pen and ink. I write because I believe in literature, in the art of the novel, more than I believe in anything else. I write because it is a habit, a passion. I write because I am afraid of being forgotten. I write because I like the glory and interest that writing brings. I write to be alone. Perhaps I write because I hope to understand why I am so very, very angry at all of you, so very, very angry at everyone. I write because I like to be read. I write because once I have begun a novel, an essay, a page, I want to finish it. I write because everyone expects me to write. I write because I have a childish belief in the immortality of libraries, and in the ways my books sit on the shelf. I write because it is exciting to turn all of life's beauties and riches into words. I write not to tell a story, but to compose a story. I write because I wish to escape from the foreboding that there is a place I must go but − just as in a dream − I can't quite get there. I write because I have never managed to be happy. I write to be happy.

Figure 1.1.1 Reasons for writing.

Excerpt from the Nobel Lecture, 'My father's suitcase' by Orhan Pamuk, translated from Turkish by Maureen Freely. Reproduced with permission of the Nobel Foundation. © The Nobel Foundation, 2006.

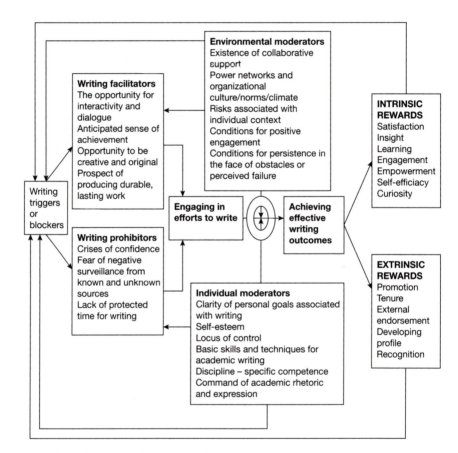

Figure 1.1.2 A social model of academic writing.

From Murray and Moore (2006), p. 179. Reproduced with permission of the authors and the Open University Press Publishing Company.

POSTSCRIPT 1: PROBLEMS FOR NON-NATIVE SPEAKERS OF ENGLISH

The IMRAD format is helpful for non-native speakers and writers, in the sense that anything that has a structure is easier to deal with than anything that has not. Unfortunately, it is more difficult for non-native speakers of English to read and to write in the appropriate style than it is for native speakers. Regrettably, methods of automatic translation have not yet progressed sufficiently for us to be able to turn scientific articles written in different languages into formal scientific English. Automated grammar and style checkers may help, but, in my experience, writers already need to have a good knowledge of grammar and style before they can judge the validity of many of the automated suggestions (Hartley *et al.*, 2007).

In my view, non-native writers of English are best aided in their writing by working with native speakers of English in their own discipline. Native speakers are more aware of the subtleties and nuances that might escape their non-native English speaking colleagues. There is a case, therefore, for more international collaboration and assistance when authors with different nationalities are involved. Fortunately, such assistance is much easier today via email and the Internet.

POSTSCRIPT 2: ONE STYLE FOR ALL . . .

I have argued in this chapter for a more readable approach to academic writing. However, these views are not shared by all. Consider, for example, the following quotations from the referees of two of my papers. If, as a writer, you are unsure about how to proceed in terms of clarity, it may be best to play it safe until you are an established author!

Paper 1

> Articles in this journal are not typically written in the first person. Whilst this may make the manuscript somewhat more accessible for some readers, it is not appropriate for a formal, academic professional outlet such as this one. In addition, the tone of the manuscript is far too informal for this journal.
>
> (Referee 1)

> This is an exceptional paper. It is 40 years since the one occasion on which I listened to Jim Hartley's voice, and I cannot recall how he sounded. Yet in this paper the writer speaks out to the reader quite personally, while at the same time conveying useful information, findings and thinking in a scholarly, rigorous and academic manner. This is a rare talent.
>
> (Referee 2)

Paper 2

The use of first person in this manuscript is a major distraction. Although the first person is acceptable if used judiciously, the word 'I' appears so much in this manuscript that the implication is that the author is more important than the research ... The manuscript must be rewritten to reduce the personal references. The present manuscript is simply so self-indulgent and so incredibly poorly presented that in-depth evaluation of the content and the meaning of the work is impossible.

(Referee 1)

This is well presented, crisp and clear. I would prefer removal of the first person at the beginning, leading to a more scholarly presentation. Very impressive literature review.

(Referee 2)

The first paper was accepted for publication: the second paper was not.

REFERENCES

Chandler, D. (1995). *The act of writing: A media theory approach*. Aberystwyth: University of Wales.

Cotton, D. & Gresty, K. (2006). Reflecting on the think-aloud method for evaluating e-learning. *British Journal of Educational Technology*, 37(1), 45–54.

Coulthard, M. (2004). Author identification, idiolect, and linguistic uniqueness. *Applied Linguistics*, 25(4), 431–47.

Elbow, P. (1998). *Writing with power* (2nd edn). New York: Oxford University Press.

Flesch, R. (1948). A new readability yardstick. *Journal of Applied Psychology*, 32 (June), 221–3.

Fowler, H. W. & Fowler, F. (1906). *The King's English*. Oxford: Clarendon Press.

Ghiselin, B. (Ed.). (1980). *The creative process: A symposium*. Berkeley, CA: University of California Press.

Graham, S. (2006). Strategy instruction and the teaching of writing: A meta-analysis. In C.A. MacArthur, S. Graham & J. Fitzgerald (Eds.), *Handbook of writing research* (pp. 187–207). New York: Guilford Press.

Hartley, J. (1994). Three ways to improve the clarity of abstracts. *British Journal of Educational Psychology*, 64(2), 331–43.

Hartley, J., Branthwaite, J. A., Ganier, F. & Heurley, L. (2007). Lost in translation: Contributions of translators to the meanings of text. *Journal of Information Science*, 35(5), 551–65.

Hartley, J., Howe, M. J. A. & McKeachie, W. J. (2001). Writing through time: Longitudinal studies of the effects of new technology on writing. *British Journal of Educational Technology*, 32(2), 141–51.

Hartley, J., Pennebaker, J. W. & Fox, C. (2003). Abstracts, introductions and discussions: How far do they differ in style? *Scientometrics*, 57(3), 389–98.

Hartley, J., Sotto, E. & Fox, C. (2004). Clarity across the disciplines: An analysis of texts in the sciences, social sciences, and arts and humanities. *Science Communication*, *26*(2), 188–210.

Hartley, J, Sotto, E. & Pennebaker, J. (2002). Style and substance in psychology: Are influential articles more readable than less influential ones? *Social Studies of Science*, *32*(2), 321–34.

Hartley, J., Trueman, M. & Meadows, A. J. (1988). Readability and prestige in scientific journals. *Journal of Information Science*, *14*(1), 69–75.

Hayes, J. R. (2006). New directions in writing research. In C.A. MacArthur, S. Graham & J. Fitzgerald (Eds.), *Handbook of writing research* (pp. 28–40). New York: Guilford Press.

Kieft, M. (2006). *The effects of adapting writing instruction to students' writing strategies*. Amsterdam: University of Amsterdam.

Klare, G. R. (1963). *The measurement of readability*. Ames, Iowa: Iowa State University Press.

Kollberg, P. & Eklundh, K. S. (2001). Studying writers' revising patterns with S-notation analysis. In T. Olive & C. M. Levy (Eds.), *Contemporary tools and techniques for studying writing* (pp. 89–104). Dordrecht: Kluwer.

Medawar, P. (1964). Is the scientific paper a fraud? Retrieved 24 September 2006 from http://bioq.weblog.com/pt/arquivo/medawar.pdf.

Murray, R. & Moore, S. (2006). *The handbook of academic writing: A fresh approach*. Maidenhead: Open University Press.

Oppenheimer, D. M. (2005). Consequences of erudite vernacular utilized irrespective of necessity: Problems with using long words needlessly. *Applied Cognitive Psychology*, *20*(2), 139–56.

Pamuk, O. (2006). My father's suitcase. Nobel lecture, 7 December 2006. Retrieved 3 January 2007 from http://nobelprize.org.nobel_prizes/literature/laureates/2006/pamuk-lecture_en.html.

Pennebaker, J. W., Francis, M. E. & Booth, R. J. (2001). *Linguistic inquiry and word count: LIWC*. Mahwah, NJ: Erlbaum.

Reid, D. J., Briggs, N. & Beveridge, M. (1983). The effects of pictures upon the readability of a school science topic. *British Journal of Educational Psychology*, *53*(3), 327–35.

Schriver, K. A. (1989). Evaluating text quality. *IEEE Transactions on Professional Communication*, *32*(4), 238–55.

Sharples, M. (1999). *How we write*. London: Routledge.

Shelley, M. & Schuh, J. H. (2001). Are the best higher education journals really the best? A meta-analysis of writing quality and readability. *Journal of Scholarly Publishing*, *33*(1), 11–22.

Smyth, T. R. (1996). *Writing in psychology: A student guide*. New York: Wiley.

Smyth. T. R. (2004). *The principles of writing in psychology:* London: Palgrave Macmillan.

Sokal, A. D. (1996). Transgressing the boundaries: Towards a transformative hermeneutics of quantum gravity. *Social Text*, *46/47* (Spring/Summer), 217–52.

Torrance, M. & Galbraith, D. (2006). The processing demands of writing. In C.A. MacArthur, S. Graham & J. Fitzgerald (Eds.), *Handbook of writing research* (pp. 67–80). New York: Guilford Press.

Torrance, M., Thomas, G. V. & Robinson, E. J. (1994). The writing strategies of graduate researchers in the social sciences. *Higher Education*, *27*, 379–92.

Watson, J. D. & Crick, F. H. C. (1953). A structure for deoxyribose nucleic acid. *Nature, 171* (25 April), 737–8.

Wellington, J. (2003). *Getting published: A guide for lecturers and researchers.* London: Routledge.

Wengelin, A. (2007). The word-level focus in text production by adults with reading and writing difficulties. In M. Torrance, L. van Waes & D. Galbraith (Eds.), *Writing and cognition: Research and applications* (pp. 67–82). Amsterdam: Elsevier.

Woods, P. (1999). *Successful writing for qualitative researchers.* London: Routledge.

FURTHER READING

Cronin, B. (2005). *The hand of science.* Lanham, MD: Scarecrow Press.

Elbow, P. (2000). *Everyone can write: Essays towards a hopeful theory of writing and teaching writing.* Oxford: Oxford University Press.

Swales, J. M. & Feak, C. B (2004). *Academic writing for graduate students: A course for non-native speakers of English* (2nd edn). Ann Arbor, Michigan, MI: University of Michigan Press.

Thaiss, C. & Zawacki, T. M. (2006). *Engaged writers and academic disciplines.* Portsmouth, NH: Boynton/Cook Publishers.

Section 2

The academic article

Titles

All articles begin with a title. Most include an abstract. Several include 'key words'. All three of these features describe an article's content in varying degrees of detail and abstraction. The title is designed to stimulate the reader's interest. The abstract summarises the content. The half-dozen or so key words, sometimes called 'descriptors', together with the title and the abstract, facilitate computer-based search and retrieval.

Although, logically, it seems sensible to start by discussing the title, it is when finishing an article that authors need to attend to it more assiduously. No doubt throughout all the drafting and preparation there will have been a working title (and a suitable journal) in mind, and, probably, this title will have changed every so often as better ways of conveying what the paper is about have come to mind. But now, at the end, it is the time to finalise it.

A good title should attract and inform the readers and be accurate. It needs to stand out in some way from the other thousands of titles that compete for the reader's attention, but it also needs to tell the reader what the paper is about. Furthermore, as the success of many computer-based searches depends upon the title, it is important to include in it some of the key words relating to the topic of the paper.

Titles come in many forms (see Crosby, 1976). Here are thirteen types that I have used, or seen used, in journal articles (Hartley, 2007). Each has advantages and disadvantages.

THIRTEEN TYPES OF TITLE

1 Titles that announce the general subject, for example:
   - The age of adolescence.
   - Designing instructional and informational text.
   - On writing scientific articles in English.
2 Titles that particularise a specific theme following a general heading, for example:

- Pre-writing: The relation between thinking and feeling.
- The achievement of black Caribbean girls: Good practice in Lambeth schools.
- The role of values in educational research: The case for reflexivity.

3 Titles that indicate the controlling question, for example:
- Is academic writing masculine?
- What is evidence-based practice – and do we want it too?
- What price presentation? The effects of typographic variables on essay grades.

4 Titles that just state the findings, for example:
- Supramaximal inflation improves lung compliance in patients with amyotrophic lateral sclerosis.
- Asthma in schoolchildren is greater in schools close to concentrated animal feeding operations.
- Angiopoetin-2 levels are elevated in exudative pleural effusions.

5 Titles that indicate that the answer to a question will be revealed, for example:
- Abstracts, introductions and discussions: How far do they differ in style?
- The effects of summaries on the recall of information.
- Current findings from research on structured abstracts.

6 Titles that announce the thesis – i.e. indicate the direction of the author's argument, for example:
- The lost art of conversation.
- Plus ça change . . . Gender preferences for academic disciplines.
- Down with 'op. cit.'.

7 Titles that emphasise the methodology used in the research, for example:
- Using colons in titles: A meta-analytic review.
- Reading and writing book reviews across the disciplines: A survey of authors.
- Is judging text on screen different from judging text in print? A naturalistic email study.

8 Titles that suggest guidelines and/or comparisons, for example:
- Seven types of ambiguity.
- Nineteen ways to have a viva.
- Eighty ways of improving instructional text.

9 Titles that bid for attention by using startling or effective openings, for example:
- 'Do you ride an elephant' and 'never tell them you're German': The experiences of British Asian, black and overseas student teachers in the UK.
- Something more to tell you: Gay, lesbian and bisexual young people's experiences of secondary schooling.
- Making a difference: An exploration of leadership roles in sixth form colleges.

10 Titles that attract by alliteration, for example:
   - A taxonomy of titles.
   - Legal ease and 'legalese'.
   - Referees are not always right: The case of the 3-D graph.
11 Titles that attract by using literary or biblical allusions, for example:
   - From structured abstracts to structured articles: A modest proposal.
   - Low! They came to pass. The motivations of failing students.
   - Lifting the veil on the viva: The experiences of postgraduate students.
12 Titles that attract by using puns, for example:
   - Now take this PIL (Patient Information Leaflet).
   - A thorn in the Flesch: Observations on the unreliability of computer-based readability formulae (Rudolph Flesch devised a method of computing the readability of text).
   - Unjustified experiments in typographical design (Text set with equal word-spacing and a ragged right-hand edge is said to be set 'unjustified': text set with variable word-spacing and a straight right-hand edge is set 'justified'.)
13 Finally, titles that mystify, for example:
   - Outside the whale.
   - How do you know you've alternated?
   - Is October Brown Chinese?

Titles that mystify may attract the indulgent reader but they are hardly likely to help busy ones. 'Outside the whale' refers to the fact that the author is describing a typographic design course that was run for over 20 years independently of, and not swallowed up by, the requirements of fine arts schools in the UK. 'How do you know you've alternated?' is about problems that sociologists have when alternating between presenting an accurate description of the groups they study, and presenting their interpretation to the readers. October Brown turns out to be the name of a school teacher.

Irony, puns, humour, and literary and cultural references are difficult for non-native speakers of the language to understand. They are probably best avoided in the titles of academic articles. So too are titles containing acronyms – abbreviations accepted as words, for example 'Mental health for IAG providers' (IAG stands for information, advice and guidance) – and neologisms – words invented to describe a new phenomenon.

GRAMMATICAL CONSTRUCTIONS IN TITLES

Soler (2007) examined 570 titles used in articles in the biological and social sciences. Some 480 of these were from research papers, and 90 from reviews. Soler distinguished between:

- full-sentence constructions, for example 'Learning induces a CDC2-related protein kinase';
- nominal group constructions, for example 'Acute liver failure caused by diffuse hepatic melanoma infiltration';
- compound constructions (i.e. divided into two parts, mainly by a colon), for example 'Romanian nominalizations: case and aspectual structure'; and
- question constructions, for example 'Does the Flynn effect affect IQ scores of students classified as learning-disabled?'.

Table 2.1.1 shows the percentage of titles in each construction for the research and the review papers categorised in terms of:

(a) the sciences
(b) the social sciences.

It can be seen that full-sentence constructions only occurred in the science research papers. Nominal group constructions were the most popular form of title, and their usage was relatively constant across the disciplines. Compound constructions were less frequent, but more common in social science research papers. Finally, questions were hardly used at all.

Table 2.1.1 The average percentage occurrence of title formats for research and review papers in articles in (a) medicine, biology and bio-chemistry, and (b) linguistics, psychology and anthropology

Titles in research papers		*Titles in review papers*	
Full-sentence construction		Full-sentence construction	
(a)	38	(a)	0
(b)	0	(b)	0
Nominal group construction		Nominal group construction	
(a)	42	(a)	55
(b)	38	(b)	55
Compound construction		Compound construction	
(a)	10	(a)	37
(b)	38	(b)	33
Question construction		Question construction	
(a)	0	(a)	4
(b)	2	(b)	13

Data adapted from Soler (2007), Tables 3–6. Reproduced with permission of the author and Elsevier Ltd.

CONCLUDING COMMENTS

Writing a good title is not easy. Table 2.1.2 shows, for example, the original titles proposed by nine final-year psychology students for their projects, followed by what I believe to be more informative ones. Most of the changes expand and clarify the originals. Readers may judge for themselves whether or not they think the revised versions will better attract and inform the readers.

Table 2.1.2 Titles used by students for their projects (in the left-hand column) and revised versions (on the right)

Approach to study (Chinese student)	Gender and nationality differences in approaches to study: Findings from English and Chinese Business Studies students
Perceptions of psychology university students	Do psychology students' perceptions of Psychology change over time?
An investigation into mature students, revision styles, and examination performance	Revision styles and examination performance in mature and traditional-entry students
Possible gender and year of study differences in the orientation of students' learning strategies	Students' learning strategies: the effects of gender and year of study
Parenting styles and academic achievement	Do differences in early parenting styles affect the academic achievement of men and women undergraduates?
University students' estimations of occupational intelligence versus gender	How intelligent do you need to be to be a surgeon? Male and female students' estimates of the intelligence required to carry out male, female and gender-neutral occupations
The effect of term-time employment on final year university students	The effects of term-time employment upon the academic performance of final-year university students
Student preferences of class size in higher education	Class size matters! The preferences of undergraduates
Students experiences of studying Psychology at degree level: Is there a difference between those that have previously studied the subject at A-level and those who have not?	How far does studying Psychology at A-level impact upon the experiences and performance of Psychology students at university?

Reproduced with permission from *Journal of Technical Writing & Communication*, 37, 1 (2007), p. 99. © Baywood Publishing Company.

REFERENCES

Crosby, H. H. (1976). Titles, a treatise on . . . *College Composition & Communication*, 27(4), 387–91.

Hartley, J. (2007). There's more to titles than meets the eye: Exploring the possibilities. *Journal of Technical Writing and Communication*, 37(1), 97–103.

Soler, V. (2007). Writing titles in science: An exploratory study. *English for Specific Purposes*, 26(1), 90–102.

FURTHER READING

Hartley, J. (2005). To attract or to inform: What are titles for? *Journal of Technical Writing and Communication*, 35(2), 203–13.

Hartley, J. Planning that title: Practices and preferences for titles with colons. *Library & Information Science Research*, 29(4), 553–68.

Authors

Providing the name of a single author is no problem. Providing the name of a pair of authors might require resolution in terms of who comes first. The problem gets more difficult as the number of authors increases.

The American Psychological Association (APA) *Publication Manual* (2001) gives clear advice on allocating credit for authorship. It states (pp. 395–6) that:

- The sequence of names of the authors to an article must reflect the relative scientific or professional contribution of the authors, irrespective of their academic status.
- The general rule is that the name of the principal contributor should come first, with subsequent names in order of decreasing contribution.
- Mere possession of an institutional position on its own, such as Head of the Research team, does not justify authorship.
- A student should be listed as a principal author on any multi-authored article that is substantially based on the student's dissertation or thesis.

However, the APA *Publication Manual* refers – in the main – to social science publications. In the sciences, the number of authors on individual papers can be very large and this can cause problems (Buehring *et al.*, 2007). One solution has been to list in more detail the contribution of each individual author to a multi-authored paper. Thus, a typical footnote might read:

> *Contributors*: A and B conceived of and designed the study, and C wrote the required program. D, E and F analysed and interpreted the data. A and D drafted the paper and B and E critically revised it. All of the authors approved this final version.

Different medical journals, however, have different requirements for listing the contributions of authors. This means that the same person might get credited in different ways for his or her contribution to the same paper, according to which journal it is submitted to (Ilakovac *et al.*, 2007). Some of the contributions listed by Ilakovac *et al.* include:

- conception and design of the study
- collection of the raw data
- statistical expertise/advice
- analysis and interpretation of the data
- drafting of the article
- critical revision of the article for important intellectual content
- administrative, technical and logistical support
- final approval of the article.

Normally, of course, these details may not matter. What matters is the contribution of the article, not who is saying it, but in these days of impact factors and citation analyses, details such as these are seen as important.

REFERENCES

American Psychological Association (2001). *Publication manual of the American Psychological Association* (5th edn). Washington: American Psychological Association.

Buehring, G. C., Buehring, J. E. & Gerard, P. D. (2007). Lost in citation: Vanishing visibility of senior authors. *Scientometrics*, *72*(3), 459–68.

Ilakovac, V., Fister, K., Marusic, M. & Marusic, A. (2007). Reliability of disclosure forms of authors' contributions. *Canadian Medical Association Journal*, *176*(1), 41–6.

Abstracts

The abstract, although it heads the article, is often written last, together with the title. This is partly because writers know what they have achieved, and partly because it is not easy to write an abstract. Abstracts have to summarise what has been done, sometimes in as few as 150 words.

It is easier to write an abstract if you remember that all abstracts have a basic structure. Indeed, the phrase 'structured abstracts' says it all. This kind of abstract, common in medical research journals and now appearing in many social science articles, can be adapted for most normal purposes.

STRUCTURED ABSTRACTS

Structured abstracts are typically written using five sub-headings – 'background', 'aim', 'method', 'results' and 'conclusions'. Sometimes the wording of these sub-headings varies a little – 'objectives' for 'aim', for example, but the meaning is much the same.

Structured abstracts were introduced into medical research journals in the 1980s. Since then they have been widely used in medicine and other areas of research (Nakayama *et al.*, 2005). In 2004, I published a narrative review of their effectiveness based upon thirty-one research papers available at that time (Hartley, 2004). I concluded that, compared with traditional abstracts, structured abstracts:

- contained more information
- were easier to read
- were easier to search
- facilitated peer review for conferences
- were generally welcomed by readers and by authors.

Figure 2.3.1a below shows a typical structured abstract. Figure 2.3.1b shows the same abstract written with the sub-headings removed. It can be seen that both abstracts are clear, and so it is useful to write an abstract in

Background. In 1997 four journals published by the British Psychological Society began publishing structured abstracts.

Aims. The aim of the studies reported here was to assess the effects of these structured abstracts by comparing them with original versions written in a traditional, unstructured format.

Method. The authors of the articles accepted for publication in the four journals were asked to supply copies of their traditional abstracts (written when the paper was submitted for publication) together with copies of their structured abstracts requested by the editor when their paper was accepted. Forty-eight such requests were made, and thirty pairs of abstracts were obtained. The abstracts were then compared on a number of measures.

Results. Analysis showed that the structured abstracts were significantly more readable, significantly longer and significantly more informative than the traditional ones. Judges assessed the contents of the structured abstracts more quickly and with significantly less difficulty than they did the traditional ones. Almost every respondent expressed positive attitudes to structured abstracts.

Conclusions. The structured abstracts fared significantly better than the traditional ones on every measure used in this enquiry. We recommend, therefore, that editors of other journals in the social sciences consider adopting structured abstracts.

Figure 2.3.1a An original abstract in structured form.

Adapted from Hartley and Benjamin (1998), and reproduced with permission of the British Journal of Educational Psychology. © the British Psychological Society.

a structured form first, and then to adjust it for the journal you are writing for if this journal does not use them.

Figures 2.3.1a and b illustrate some of the virtues of structured abstracts. Using the sub-headings and the appropriately spaced typographical layout makes the content clearer (Hartley and Betts, 2007). Furthermore, structured abstracts are easier for readers to scan, as every abstract follows the same format. The sub-headings thus allow the readers to go to the same place each time in an abstract to find out what it says. Furthermore, as the information required has to be provided by the author under each sub-heading, nothing gets missed out. With traditional abstracts, it is all too common to find that some elements are missing – the background, the method or the results, for example. Often one is left saying, 'So, what happened?' or 'So what?'.

In 1997 four journals published by the British Psychological Society began publishing structured abstracts. The aim of the studies reported here was to assess the effects of these structured abstracts by comparing them with original versions written in a traditional, unstructured format. The authors of the articles accepted for publication in the four journals were asked to supply copies of their traditional abstracts (written when the paper was submitted for publication) together with copies of their structured abstracts requested by the editor when their paper was accepted. Forty-eight such requests were made and thirty pairs of abstracts were obtained. The abstracts were then compared on a number of measures. Analysis showed that the structured abstracts were significantly more readable, significantly longer and significantly more informative than the traditional ones. Judges assessed the contents of the structured abstracts more quickly and with significantly less difficulty than they did the traditional ones. Almost every respondent expressed positive attitudes to structured abstracts. In short, the structured abstracts fared significantly better than the traditional ones on every measure used in this enquiry. We recommend, therefore, that editors of other journals in the social sciences consider adopting structured abstracts.

Figure 2.3.1b The same abstract in unstructured form.

Many people think that structured abstracts are only suitable for empirical papers – those with 'methods' and 'results'. As one of my correspondents put it:

> It seems to me that the format you have chosen imposes a unitary conception of research, at a time when educational research in particular, and social science more widely, has at last broken away from narrow strictures of method and procedure.

However, I believe that the underlying characteristics of a structured abstract can apply to many other forms of enquiry. Figure 2.3.2a, for example, shows an original abstract written to accompany a review paper. Figure 2.3.2b shows a revision of it that, in my view, makes the background, aims and conclusions of the study more explicit.

Bayley and Eldredge (2003) provide references to a variety of papers in the health sciences that have structured abstracts. These include qualitative studies, narrative reviews, systematic reviews, meta-analyses and randomised controlled trials. Table 2.3.1 similarly lists some more recent papers in the

There is something of a controversy taking place over how best to theorise human learning. In this article we join the debate over the relationships between sociocultural and constructive perspectives on learning. These two perspectives differ in not just their conceptions of knowledge (epistemological assumptions) but also in their assumptions about the known world and the knowing human (ontological assumptions). We articulate in this article six themes of a nondualist ontology seen at work in the sociocultural perspective, and suggest a reconciliation of the two. We propose that learning involves becoming a member of a community, constructing knowledge of various levels of expertise as a participant, but also taking a stand on the culture of one's community in an effort to take up and overcome the estrangement and division that are consequences of participation. Learning entails transformation of both the person and the social world. We explore the implications of this view for thinking about schooling and for the conduct of educational research.

Figure 2.3.2a An original abstract for a review paper.

Reproduced with permission from Packer and Goicoechea (2000) and Taylor & Francis, www. informaworld.com.

health and social sciences that have used structured abstracts with a variety of research methods.

After the title, the abstract is the most frequently read part of any paper. Writing it in a structured format (with or without the headings) ensures that it is informative and complete.

Table 2.3.1 Examples of studies with structured abstracts published in the health and social sciences

Method	Example
Literature review	Mayhew and Simpson (2002)
Observational study	Lauth et al. (2006)
Survey	Wilding and Andrews (2006)
Longitudinal study	Flouri (2006)
Statistical paper	Prosser and Trigwell (2006)
Simulation	Wright (2006)
Experimental study	Clariana and Koul (2006)
Epidemiological study	Evans (2000)
Meta-analysis	Bunn et al. (2006)
Systematic review	Duperrex et al. (2006)
Qualitative study	Maliski et al. (2002)

Background. An interesting debate is currently taking place among proponents of different ways of thinking about human learning. In this article we focus on that portion of the debate that addresses sociological and constructive perspectives on learning. These two perspectives differ in not just their conceptions of knowledge (epistemological assumptions) but also in their assumptions about the known world and the knowing human (ontological assumptions).

Aims and approach. We wish to try and reconcile these two different approaches first by examining the ontological assumptions of them both. We then consider six key themes of a nondualist ontology seen at work in the sociocultural perspective. Finally we propose that the constructive perspective attends to epistemological structures and processes which the sociological perspective must place in a broader historical and cultural context.

Conclusions. We conclude that learning involves becoming a member of a community, constructing knowledge of various levels of expertise as a participant, and taking a stand on the culture of one's community in an effort to take up and overcome the estrangement and division that are consequences of participation. Learning entails transformation of both the personal and the social world. We explore the implications of this view for thinking about schooling and the conduct of educational research.

Figure 2.3.2b The same abstract in structured form.

REFERENCES

Bayley, L. & Eldredge, J. E. (2003). The structured abstract: An essential tool for researchers. *Hypothesis, 17*(1), 1 and 11–15. Or: http://research.mlanet.org/structured_abstract.html. (Retrieved 1 August 2006.)

Bunn, F., Collier, T., Frost, C., Ker, K., Roberts, I. & Wentz, R. (2003). Traffic calming for the prevention of road traffic injuries: Systematic review and meta-analysis. *Injury Prevention, 9*(3), 200–4.

Clariana, R. B. & Koul, R. (2006). The effects of different forms of feedback on fuzzy and verbatim memory of science principles. *British Journal of Educational Psychology, 76*(2), 259–70.

Duperrex, O., Bunn, F. & Roberts, I. (2002). Safety education of pedestrians for injury prevention: A systematic review of randomised controlled trials. *British Medical Journal, 324*(7348), 1129–34.

Evans, L. (2000). Risks older drivers face themselves and threats they pose to other road users. *International Journal of Epidemiology, 29*(2), 315–22.

Flouri, E. (2006). Parental interest in children's education, children's self-esteem and locus of control, and later educational attainment: Twenty-six year follow-up of the 1970 British Birth Cohort. *British Journal of Educational Psychology*, 76(1), 41–56.

Hartley, J. (2004). Current findings from research on structured abstracts. *Journal of the Medical Library Association*, 92(3), 368–71.

Hartley, J. & Benjamin, M. (1998). An evaluation of structured abstracts in journals published by the British Psychological Society. *British Journal of Educational Psychology*, 68(3), 443–56.

Hartley, J. & Betts, L. (2007). The effects of spacing and titles on judgments of the effectiveness of structured abstracts. *Journal of the American Society for Information Science & Technology*, 58(14), 2335–40.

Lauth, G. W., Heubeck, B. G. & Maçkowiak, K. (2006). Observation of children with attention-deficit hyperactivity (ADHD) problems in three natural classroom contexts. *British Journal of Educational Psychology*, 76(2), 385–404.

Maliski, S. L., Heilemann, M. V. & McCorkle, R. (2002). From 'death sentence' to 'good cancer': Couples' transformation of a prostate cancer diagnosis. *Nursing Research*, 5(6), 391–7.

Mayhew, D. R. & Simpson, H. M. (2002). The safety value of driver education and training. *Injury Prevention*, 8 (Suppl. II): ii3-ii8.

Nakayama, T., Hirai, N., Yamazaki, S. & Naito, M. (2005). Adoption of structured abstracts by general medical journals and format for a structured abstract. *Journal of the Medical Library Association*, 93(2), 237–42.

Packer, M. J. & Goicoechea, J. (2000). Sociocultural and constructivist theories of learning: Ontological, not just epistemology. *Educational Psychologist*, 35(4), 227–41.

Prosser, M. & Trigwell, K. (2006). Confirmatory factor analysis of the Approaches to Teaching Inventory. *British Journal of Educational Psychology*, 76(2), 405–19.

Wilding, J. & Andrews, B. (2006). Life goals, approaches to study and performance in an undergraduate cohort. *British Journal of Educational Psychology*, 76(1), 171–82.

Wright, D. B. (2006). Comparing groups in a before-after design: When *t* test and ANCOVA produce different results. *British Journal of Educational Psychology*, 76(3), 663–75.

FURTHER READING

Hartley, J., Rock, J. & Fox, C. (2005). Teaching psychology students to write structured abstracts: An evaluation study. *Psychology Teaching Review*, 1(1), 2–11.

Kamler, B. & Thomson, P. (2004). Driven to abstraction: Doctoral supervision and writing pedagogies. *Teaching in Higher Education*, 9(2), 195–209.

Kelly, A. E. & Yin, R. K. (2007). Strengthening structured abstracts for education research: The need for claim-based structured abstracts. *Educational Researcher*, 36(3), 133–8.

Key words

Key words typically:

1 allow readers to judge whether or not an article contains material relevant to their interests;
2 provide readers with suitable terms to use in web-based searches to locate other materials on the same or similar topics;
3 help indexers/editors group together related materials in, say, the end-of-year issues of a particular journal or a set of conference proceedings;
4 allow editors/researchers to document changes in a subject discipline (over time); and
5 link the specific issues of concern to issues at a higher level of abstraction.

WHO USES KEY WORDS?

There appear to be no formal requirements for key words, no rules for formulating them, little guidance on how to write them, and no instructions for reviewers on how to assess them. This is surprising in view of the fact that, presumably, a wise choice of key words increases the probability that a paper will be retrieved and read, thereby potentially improving citation counts and journal impact factors. Table 2.4.1 shows, however, that there are typical disciplinary differences in the percentage of journals using key words.

Table 2.4.1 The approximate percentages of research journals in different areas and disciplines supplying key words

Arts	Education	Psychology	Science	Medicine	Statistics
5	20	30	50	50	75

Hartley and Kostoff (2003).

WHO CHOOSES THE KEY WORDS?

Table 2.4.2 shows that there are several different ways of choosing key words. The most common method (used by over fifty per cent of authors) is for them to supply as many words as they choose (within bounds), but sometimes a specified number of words is required (often about six). The next main method (used by about twenty per cent of authors) is for them to choose key words that fit into categories already prescribed by the journal's 'instructions to authors'. Thus, for example, authors generating key words for medical articles often have to select only words from the medical subject headings (MeSH) taxonomy – a structured taxonomy used by MEDLINE. In situations like this the number of words allowed and the number of categories to choose from can vary. Many psychology journals, for example, ask authors to list key words from any of the 5,000 terms that appear in the American Psychological Society's *Thesaurus of Psychological Index Terms*. Finally, key words are sometimes generated automatically at proof stage (as is the case for the *Journal of Information Science*, where the key words are derived from *Library and Information Science Abstracts*).

HOW TO SELECT KEY WORDS

Gbur and Trumbo (1995) published a list of ways of producing effective key words and phrases. Table 2.4.3 provides an abbreviated version.

It is possible that, with future developments, all of these problems will actually disappear. As one colleague has put it, 'Inverted-full-text-Boolean indexing and online searching (with similarity algorithms and citation-

Table 2.4.2 Different methods for supplying key words

Authors supply them with no restrictions on the numbers allowed.

Authors supply up to a fixed number (e.g. six).

Authors supply key words as appropriate from a specified list.

Editors supplement/amend authors' key words.

Editors supply key words.

Editors supply key words from a specified list.

Referees supply key words from a specified list.

Key words are allocated according to the 'house-rules' applied to all journals distributed by a specific publisher.

Key words are determined by computer program at proof stage.

Hartley and Kostoff (2003).

Table 2.4.3 Ten ways to produce effective key words and phrases

1	Use simple, specific noun clauses. For example, use *variance estimation*, not *estimate of variance*.
2	Avoid terms that are too common. Otherwise the number of 'hits' will be too large to manage.
3	Do not repeat key words from the title. These will be picked up anyway.
4	Avoid unnecessary prepositions, especially *in* and *of*. For example, use *data quality* rather than *quality of data*.
5	Avoid acronyms. Acronyms can fall out of favour and be puzzling to beginners and/or overseas readers.
6	Spell out Greek letters and avoid mathematical symbols. These are impractical for computer-based searches.
7	Include only the names of people if they are part of an established terminology, for example *Skinner box*, *Poisson distribution*.
8	Include, where applicable, mathematical or computer techniques, such as *generating function*, used to derive results, and a statistical philosophy or approach such as *maximum likelihood* or *Bayes' theory*.
9	Include alternative or inclusive terminology. If a concept is, or has been, known by different terminologies, use a key word that might help a user conducting a search across a time-span, or from outside your speciality. For example, the statistician's *characteristic function* is the mathematician's *Fourier transform*, and in some countries *educational administration* is *educational management*.
10	Note areas of applications where appropriate.

Adapted from Gbur and Trumbo (1995), pp. 29–33, and reproduced in substantially altered form with permission of the authors and *The American Statistician*. © the American Statistical Association, 1995. All rights reserved.

ranking) will soon make keywords and human-subject-classification a thing of the past'. Put more simply, this means that we will soon be able to input any words, pairs of words or phrases that we like from an article into a search engine and come up with related materials. Unfortunately, of course, this also means that the searcher is likely to be swamped with information – most of which will be inappropriate. If, for example, you use Google Advanced Scholar to search for 'key words', you will obtain approximately 800 citations.

All of this suggests that considerable thought needs to go into the selection of key words. Borrowing from Hughes (2005), it might be worth considering selecting words from a series of categories such as:

- discipline: for example economics, management, psychology, education
- method: for example experiment, case study, questionnaire, grounded theory
- data source: for example primary, secondary, tertiary students, senior citizens
- location: for example country, town, institution
- topic: for example academic writing.

REFERENCES

Gbur, E. E. & Trumbo, B. (1995). Key words and phrases – the key to scholarly visibility and efficiency in an information explosion. *The American Statistician*, *49*(1), 29–33.

Hartley, J. & Kostoff, R. N. (2003). How useful are 'key words' in scientific journals? *Journal of Information Science*, *29*(5), 433–8.

Hughes, W. P. (2005). Keywords: Their choice and their importance. *Association of Researchers in Construction Management (ARCOM) Newsletter*, *20*(1), 2–3 and *21*(1), 4–5.

Introductions

It is but a short step from structured abstracts to structured texts. In the following chapters we shall see how each part of the structure of a scientific article (the introduction, method, results, discussion and conclusion) can indeed be subdivided into finer structures.

Swales and Feak (2004) describe what they characterise as 'moves' in the various sections of academic articles. Basically, a 'move' is a stage in the argument that all writers go through. The 'moves' for the introduction are typically as follows (p. 244):

- *Move 1*: The authors establish a research territory:
  - (a) by showing that the general research area is important, central, interesting, problematic or relevant in some way (optional);
  - (b) by introducing and reviewing items of previous research in the area (obligatory).
- *Move 2*: They then establish a 'niche' by indicating a weakness in the account so far:
  - (a) by indicating a gap in the previous research, raising a question about it or extending previous knowledge in some way (obligatory).
- *Move 3*: They then occupy the niche by saying they are going to put this right:
  - (a) by outlining the purposes or stating the nature of the present research (obligatory);
  - (b) by listing research questions or hypotheses to be tested (optional);
  - (c) by announcing the principal findings (optional).

Swales and Feak argue that most introductions to academic articles follow this basic structure. Lewin *et al.* (2001) offer a similar, but more detailed, analysis that readers might also find useful.

AN EXAMPLE

While writing this section of *Academic Writing and Publishing*, I coincidentally received a copy of a paper by Slatcher and Pennebaker (2006). This paper was about the effects of one of the partners of a dating couple writing either neutral or strongly emotional letters to the other one about their relationship. The paper concluded that the participants who wrote the emotional letters were significantly more likely to be dating their romantic partners three months later than were the writers of the neutral letters. Be that as it may, I was intrigued to observe that the introduction to this paper followed almost exactly the generic structure described by Swales and Feak.

Slatcher and Pennebaker's introduction contains five paragraphs. Here are some examples of how the moves appear:

Move 1: Establishing a research territory

The paper starts (paragraphs 1 and 2) with describing the background and setting the scene. Key phrases are: 'Researchers are now . . .', 'Preliminary findings suggest . . .', 'There are a number of ways in which one could measure the effects of expressive writing . . .'.

Move 2: Establishing a niche

The paper continues (in paragraphs 3 and 4) with the following key phrases: 'Although previous studies have addressed . . . none have . . .', 'One potential mediator is . . .', 'There are various ways to measure . . .', 'The use of emotional words may be particularly relevant . . .', 'One way is to analyse the texts used in instant messaging . . .'.

Move 3: Occupying the niche

The introduction concludes (in paragraph 5) with the following key phrases: 'In the present study we sought to investigate the social effects of expressive writing . . .', 'Three predictions were tested. First . . .'.

Slatcher and Pennebaker thus follow Swales and Feak's analysis almost line by line. It is also worth noting, in passing, that the literature review in this paper is quite short, and there are only nine references. Day and Gastel (2006) comment that, 'Introductions should supply sufficient information to allow the reader to understand and evaluate the results of the present study without (them) needing to refer to previous publications on the topic' (pp. 57–8).

Of course many papers are written with more detailed substructures. Three types of structure typical in introductions are:

1   The one listed above – where the authors establish their niche by indicating limitations or omissions in the previous research.

2   One where two (or more) different areas of research are reviewed – and the authors establish their niche by bringing them together.

3   One where some previous research has provided support for a particular finding or theory, and some has not – and the authors establish their niche by seeking to resolve and explain this.

Further, there are disciplinary variations: Haggan (1998), for example, examined the introductions for twenty-six articles in the sciences, twenty-six in linguistics and twenty-six in the arts. She found that the introductions in the science papers were less likely to contain a plan for the paper than were the introductions in linguistics, and that they lay midway in their use of impersonal language between introductions in the arts (the least personal) and introductions in linguistics (the most personal). Introductions in the sciences were more personal, however, when there was more than one author.

Such disciplinary formulaic introductions enhance the clarity of a paper and ensure that the readers' expectations about the format and the purpose of an introduction are maintained. Such devices keep the reader reading.

REFERENCES

Day, R. A. & Gastel, B. (2006). *How to write and publish a scientific paper* (6th edn). Cambridge: Cambridge University Press.

Haggan, M. (1998). In search of the linguistics niche: A study of research article introductions in Linguistics, Literature and Science. *Arab Journal for the Humanities*, *61*, 345–77.

Lewin, B., Fine, J. & Young, L. (2001). *Expository discourse: A genre-based approach to social science research texts*. London: Continuum.

Slatcher, R. B. & Pennebaker, J. W. (2006). How do I love thee? Let me count the words. *Psychological Science*, *17*(8), 660–4.

Swales, J. M. & Feak, C. B. (2004). *Academic writing for graduate students* (2nd edn). Ann Arbor, MI: University of Michigan Press.

FURTHER READING

Kendall, P. C., Silk, J. S. & Chu, B. C. (2000). Introducing your research report: Writing the introduction. In R. J. Sternberg (Ed.), *Guide to publishing in psychology journals* (pp. 41–57). Cambridge: Cambridge University Press.

Methods

Method sections vary in journal articles, but rather less so than introductions. This is because the 'moves' in the method sections generally involve working through a series of subsections. Most method sections are usually subdivided (with subheadings) into three sections, as follows:

1   participants
2   measures
3   procedure(s).

If no participants are involved, then the method simply describes the measures and procedure(s). In the Slatcher and Pennebaker (2006) example, there are three subheadings in the method section: Participants, Procedure and Linguistic Analysis (or measures).

Method sections may be brief and succinct – when the methods used are well known and standardised – or quite lengthy, when the methods used are new or different and thus require careful elaboration.

Students and authors are typically instructed to write their method sections in such a way that readers can repeat the method from the descriptions given. Day and Gastel (2006, p. 64) recommend that colleagues unfamiliar with what was done should be asked to read the account to see if they can follow it. Authors are sometimes too close to what they did and thus tend to forget to mention tiny but – sometimes – key details.

A useful device for clarifying the procedure or the method for the reader – especially if it is complicated – is to summarise it in a table or figure (e.g. see Gotzsche, 2006). Figure 2.6.1 gives a schematic version of Slatcher and Pennebaker's prose description of their method. Such procedures, though, are rarely used. None of the authors of fifty-six articles in the 2005 volume of the *Journal of Educational Psychology* used this strategy, and only two provided illustrations of the equipment used. However, eleven (i.e. twenty per cent) of these articles did include figures to illustrate either the theoretical models underlying the reasoning for their experiments or the analyses that they were going to use.

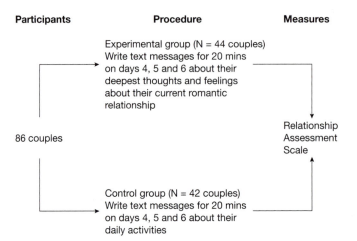

Participants	Procedure	Measures

Figure 2.6.1 A schematic illustration of the prose version of the Method used in the study by Slatcher and Pennebaker (2006).

REFERENCES

Day, R. A. & Gastel, B. (2006). *How to write and publish a scientific paper* (6th edn). Cambridge: Cambridge University Press.

Gotzsche, P. C. (2006). Believability of relative risks and odds ratios in abstracts: A cross sectional study. *British Medical Journal*, *333*, 231–4.

Slatcher, R. B. & Pennebaker, J. W. (2006). How do I love thee? Let me count the words. *Psychological Science*, *17*(8), 660–4.

FURTHER READING

Reis, H. T. (2000). Writing effectively about design. In R. J. Sternberg (Ed.), *Guide to publishing in psychology journals* (pp. 81–97). Cambridge: Cambridge University Press.

Results

A 'moves' analysis of the results sections of academic articles either looks like this:

- *Move 1*: State the main findings in order – relating them in turn to the hypotheses and methods used.
- *Move 2*: State the subsidiary findings – relating them in turn to the hypotheses and methods used.

or it is an interweaving of the two – the first set of main findings and related subsidiary ones, followed by the second set, and so on.

Again these subsections may be cued by subheadings. Slatcher and Pennebaker (2006), for example, divide their results section into two main parts (separated by the subheadings, 'Relationship stability and language use', and 'Mediation effects of changes in use of emotional words'). They provide a description of the results obtained, mainly in prose, in each part, indicating that the partners who wrote the romantic letters were significantly more likely to be dating their romantic partners three months later than were the partners who wrote the neutral ones.

It is typical in results sections to present the main data that support (or reject) the hypotheses in the form of tables and graphs. Indeed, it is quite common to find that the first sentence of a results section begins, 'Table 1 shows that . . .'. Slatcher and Pennebaker's paper is unusual here in that they provide only one such table, near the start of their second section of results, and this table is not used to illustrate their main findings. Because tables and graphs are so important in academic and scientific writing, I shall discuss them separately, in more detail, in Chapter 3.5.

Salovey (2000) argues that the art of writing a good results section is to take the readers through a story. This does not mean working step by step through the results obtained, but rather – as implied above – articulating what happened and illustrating it clearly, usually with data. In my view, this story is clearer if the sequence of topics addressed in the results section is the same as that articulated in the introduction and the method(s) sections.

Swales and Feak (2004) comment that the distinction between the results and the subsequent discussion section is not always as sharp as one might think. They cite a study by Thompson (1993) that showed that the authors of papers in biochemistry used a variety of rhetorical devices in their results section to justify their methodology, to interpret and comment on the findings, and to relate them to previous research. Indeed, the only thing that they did not do in their results sections was to call for further research – this was left for the discussion.

REFERENCES

Salovey, P. (2000). Results that get results. Telling a good story. In R. J. Sternberg (Ed.), *Guide to publishing in psychology journals* (pp. 121–32). Cambridge: Cambridge University Press.

Slatcher, R. B. & Pennebaker, J. W. (2006). How do I love thee? Let me count the words. *Psychological Science, 17*(8), 660–4.

Swales, J. M. & Feak, C. B. (2004). *Academic writing for graduate students* (2nd edn). Ann Arbor, MI: University of Michigan Press.

Thompson, D. K. (1993). Arguing for experimental 'facts' in science: A study of research article results sections in biochemistry. *Written Communication, 10*(1), 106–28.

Discussions

Discussions, like introductions, have a typical structure. Lewin *et al.* (2001) and Swales and Feak (2004) describe typical 'moves' in the discussion sections of academic research papers. Putting these descriptions together suggests the following moves:

- *Move 1*: Restate the findings and accomplishments.
- *Move 2*: Evaluate how the results fit in with the previous findings – do they contradict, qualify, agree or go beyond them?
- *Move 3*: List potential limitations to the study.
- *Move 4*: Offer an interpretation/explanation of these results and ward off counter-claims.
- *Move 5*: State the implications and recommend further research.

Discussions, then, go beyond a summary of the findings and, indeed, there may be disciplinary differences in how they are approached. Holmes (1997), for instance, found that the discussion sections of papers in sociology and political science were similar in format to those in the sciences, whereas those in history were less complex. Swales and Feak (2004) state that some scientists believe that a long discussion implies weak methods and results, whereas social scientists and people in the arts may well believe the opposite.

AN EXAMPLE

Lewin *et al.* (2001) provide numerous quotations from the discussion sections of several research articles to support the above 'moves' analysis. In terms of Slatcher and Pennebaker's (2006) paper referred to earlier, we may note the following sentences contained in the six paragraphs of their discussion section:

- *Move 1*: Restating the findings and accomplishments:
  - – Par. 1: 'The very simple act of writing about their romantic relationship changed the way in which participants communicated . . .';
  - – Par. 2: 'Taken together these findings shed light on processes underlying interactions in close relationships . . .';
  - – Par. 3: 'An advantage of the current design is that . . .';
  - – Par. 6: 'Unlike previous expressive-writing studies, this is the first to demonstrate . . .'.
- *Move 2*: Evaluating how the results fit in with previous research:
  - – Par. 3: 'In particular, the findings relating to increases in emotion words illuminate previous research [3 references provided]'.
- *Move 3*: Stating the limitations:
  - – Par. 5: 'There are some potential limitations in this study. First . . . Second . . .'.
- *Move 4*: Warding off alternative explanations:
  - – Par. 5. '. . . make this an unlikely possibility'.
- *Move 5*: Stating implications:
  - – Par. 4: . . . [this finding] 'has clear implications for clinicians';
  - – Par. 5: '. . . future studies should address this issue'.

These quotations illustrate that the five moves are present, but they are not as clearly sequenced or indicated as might be implied from the list above. Authors seem more flexible in how they tackle their discussions, although the moves listed are usually present.

Discussion sections are difficult to write because their aim is to discuss and comment on the findings, rather than just to report them. Day and Gastel (2006) suggest that journal editors reject many papers because of their weak discussions. They recommend that discussions should end with a short summary regarding the significance of the work, which, they claim, is not always adequately considered.

Woods (1999) recommends:

1   that writers should keep notes about what it might be useful to include in the discussion as ideas occur to them when they are writing other sections; and
2   that it might be wise to set aside a day or two to tackle this section of the paper.

This, he says, will make the task less daunting.

REFERENCES

Day, R. A. & Gastel, B. (2006). *How to write and publish a scientific paper* (6th edn). Cambridge: Cambridge University Press.

Holmes, R. (1997). Genre analysis, and the social sciences: An investigation of the structure of research article discussion sections in three disciplines. *English for Specific Purposes*, *16*(4), 321–37.

Lewin, B., Fine, J. & Young, L. (2001). *Expository discourse: A genre-based approach to social science research texts*. London: Continuum.

Slatcher, R. B. & Pennebaker, J. W. (2006). How do I love thee? Let me count the words. *Psychological Science*, *17*(8), 660–4.

Swales, J. M. & Feak, C. B. (2004). *Academic writing for graduate students* (2nd edn). Ann Arbor, MI: University of Michigan Press.

Woods, P. (1999). *Successful writing for qualitative researchers*. London: Routledge.

FURTHER READING

Calfee, R. (2000). What does it all mean? The discussion. In R. J. Sternberg (Ed.), *Guide to publishing in psychology journals* (pp. 133–45). Cambridge: Cambridge University Press.

Acknowledgements

Most academic articles contain acknowledgements to various sources of help received during their preparation, although one editor of my acquaintance steadfastly deletes them on the grounds that they add nothing to the content. However, I believe that it is courteous to thank sources of financial support and colleagues and referees for their help in improving articles. Slatcher and Pennebaker conclude:

> Portions of this research were funded by a grant from the National Institutes of Health (MH53291). We would like to thank Greg Hixon, Amy Kaderka and Girish Tembe for their assistance on this project and Amie Green, Timothy Loving, Mathew Newman, William Swann, and Simine Vazire for their helpful comments on an earlier draft of this article.
>
> (Slatcher and Pennebaker, 2006, p. 663)

Suls and Fletcher (1983) counted the acknowledgements to colleagues in papers in chemistry, physics, psychology and sociology, with the number of acknowledgements adjusted for the number of authors of the papers. (The number of joint authors was highest in physics and lowest in sociology.) Suls and Fletcher found that the proportion of acknowledgements to colleagues increased as one moved through the disciplines from chemistry to sociology.

More recently, Cronin *et al.* (2003) examined the acknowledgements in all of the several hundred articles published in the *Psychological Review* and in *Mind* from 1900 to 1999. In both journals, there was an upswing in the percentage of articles with acknowledgements – from the 1960s for *Psychological Review* and from the 1980s for *Mind* – until 1999, when almost ninety per cent of their articles contained them. Cronin *et al.* (2004) then repeated their analyses with samples from the *Journal for the American Chemical Society*. Here the upswing started earlier (in the 1940s) and over ninety per cent of the articles in this journal have contained acknowledgements since the 1960s.

Cronin *et al.* (2003) separated the different parts of an acknowledgement as follows:

- *financial* (recognition of extramural or internal funding);
- *instrumental/technical* (providing access to tools, technologies, facilities, and also furnishing technical expertise, such as statistical analysis);
- *conceptual* (source of inspiration, idea generation, critical insight, intellectual guidance, assistance of referees etc.);
- *editorial* (providing advice on manuscript preparation, submission, bibliographic assistance etc.); and
- *moral* (recognising the support of family, friends etc.).

Table 2.9.1 shows the relative proportions of these categories in the acknowledgements in the three journals examined by Cronin *et al.* (2003; 2004). These data reveal clear disciplinary differences, and they also tell us indirectly something about the intellectual debts incurred in writing a paper.

However, even *within* disciplines, a closer examination of the acknowledgements can reveal interesting things (see Cronin and Franks, 2006; Hartley, 2003). It appears, for example, that – in psychology – there are differences in the numbers of acknowledgements given by single authors compared with those given by pairs or trios of authors. In one study, for example, I examined the acknowledgements made in the *Journal of Educational Psychology*, *Teaching of Psychology* and *Psychological Science* (Hartley, 2003). Here fifty-seven per cent of single authors acknowledged the help of colleagues, referees and editors, compared with forty-nine per cent of pairs and forty per cent of trios. It appeared then that single authors benefited from discussions with other colleagues – who were acknowledged – more than did pairs or groups of writers who were perhaps in a better position to discuss salient issues among themselves.

In all of the studies described above, the authors worked by hand when counting the elements in the data. However, automated methods for analysing acknowledgements are now available and, with these, larger samples from many more journals can be considered. Giles and Councill (2004), for example,

Table 2.9.1 The proportions of acknowledgements (%) devoted to different aspects of acknowledgements in *Mind, Psychological Review* and the *Journal of the American Chemical Society*

	Mind	Psychological Review	Journal of the American Chemical Society
Financial	11	36	46
Technical	4	20	34
Conceptual	69	31	18
Editorial	11	11	1
Moral	1	–	–

Data derived from Cronin *et al.* (2003; 2004) and reproduced with permission of the authors.

carried out one such automated study of 188,052 acknowledgements in science papers. They showed that funding agencies got the highest rates of acknowledgements, commercial companies the next, educational institutions the third, and individuals the least. More interesting, perhaps, is that it will soon be relatively easy, using such computer-based techniques, to trace which people are acknowledged most in a given field, and thus to assess their currently hidden contribution, and also to see if acknowledgements to colleagues are reciprocal in different papers.

Finally, Day and Gastel (2006) remind us that it is always appropriate to check with the people named in acknowledgements that they are happy with what is said and, if necessary, to reword it in the light of their comments. Indeed, some journals require that all the people listed in the acknowledgements, as well as all the authors, each sign separate consent forms allowing publication.

REFERENCES

Cronin, B. & Franks, S. (2006). Trading cultures: Resource mobilization and service rendering in the life sciences as revealed in the journal article's paratext. *Journal of the American Society for Information Science & Technology*, 57(14), 1909–18.

Cronin, B., Shaw, D. & La Barre, K. (2003). A cast of thousands: Coauthorship and subauthorship collaboration in the 20th century as manifested in the scholarly literature of Psychology and Philosophy. *Journal of the American Society for Information Science and Technology*, 54(9), 855–71.

Cronin, B., Shaw, D. & La Barre, K. (2004). Visible, less visible and invisible work: Patterns of collaboration in 20th century Chemistry. *Journal of the American Society for Information Science and Technology*, 55(2), 160–8.

Day, R. A. & Gastel, B. (2006). *How to write and publish a scientific paper* (6th edn). Cambridge: Cambridge University Press.

Giles, C. L. & Councill, I. G. (2004). Who gets acknowledged: Measuring scientific contributions through automated acknowledgement indexing. *Proceedings of the National Academy of Sciences*, 101(51), 1759–64.

Hartley, J. (2003). Single authors are not alone: Colleagues often help. *The Journal of Scholarly Publishing*, 34(2), 108–13.

Slatcher, R. B. & Pennebaker, J. W. (2006). How do I love thee? Let me count the words. *Psychological Science*, 17(8), 660–4.

Suls, J. & Fletcher, B. (1983). Social comparison in the social and physical sciences: An archival study. *Journal of Personality and Social Psychology*, 44(3), 575–80.

FURTHER READING

Cronin, B. (1995). *The scholar's courtesy: The role of acknowledgement in the primary communication process*. London: Taylor Graham.

Cronin, B. (2005). *The hand of science: Academic writing and its rewards*. Lanham, Maryland: Scarecrow Press.

References

Many different styles of referencing have developed over the years. National standards have been agreed in the USA, UK, Europe and China. However, few publishers appear to follow these standards precisely, perhaps because they each allow some degree of choice. Today variation seems rife, and this is made worse by computer-based systems for preparing references, such as EndNote, Procite and Reference Manager. EndNote (2007) proudly boasts that it includes 'more than 2,300 predefined bibliographic styles for leading journals', although quite why anyone should want such a number is anybody's guess.

Currently there are four main styles of referencing for academic articles, as follows:

1 The APA style. This system is also known as the Harvard or, more colloquially, as the 'name(date)' system. This is because an author's surname in the text is followed by the date of the publication in brackets, and entries in the reference list are listed alphabetically, starting with the name and the initials of the author(s) followed by the date of publication for each entry. For example:

> Sharples, M. (Ed.). (1993). *Computer supported collaborative writing.* London: Springer-Verlag.
>
> Speck, B. W., Johnson, T. R., Dice, C. P., & Heaton, L. B. (1999). *Collaborative writing: An annotated bibliography.* Westport, Connecticut: Greenwood Press.
>
> Tang, C. (1998). Effects of collaborative learning on the quality of assignments. In B. Dart & G. Boulton-Lewis (Eds.), *Teaching and learning in higher education* (pp. 102–23). Melbourne: Australian Council for Educational Research.
>
> Zammuner, V. L. (1995). Individual and co-operative computer writing and revising: Who gets the best results? *Learning and Instruction*, 5(2), 101–24.

2   The Modern Languages Association (MLA) style. In this version the authors' surnames (with or without the dates) appear in the text and the first author's surname comes first in the reference list. This is followed by his or her first name, but first names then come first for any additional authors. Dates of the publications are given after journal titles, or at the end of the references for books, etc. The list is ordered alphabetically. For example:

> Sharples, Michael (Ed.). *Computer Supported Collaborative Writing.* London: Springer-Verlag, 1993.
> Speck, Bruce W., Teresa R. Johnson, Catherine Dice, and Leon B. Heaton. *Collaborative Writing: An Annotated Bibliography.* Westport, Connecticut: Greenwood Press, 1999.
> Tang, Catherine. 'Effects of collaborative learning on the quality of assignments.' *Teaching and Learning in Higher Education.* Eds. Barry Dart and Gillian Boulton-Lewis. Pp. 103–23. Melbourne: Australian Council for Educational Research, 1998.
> Zammuner, Victoria L. 'Individual and co-operative computer writing and revising: Who gets the best results?' *Learning and Instruction* 5 (1995) 101–24.

3   The Institute of Electronic and Electrical Engineers (IEEE) style. Here, the authors in the text are numbered in order of their appearance in the text, sometimes without their names, and the numbers are enclosed in square brackets. The reference list is then numbered sequentially. Names are presented with the initial(s) first, followed by surnames. Dates of the publications are given after journal titles, or at the end of the references for book, etc. Journal titles are sometimes abbreviated. For example:

> [1] M. Sharples, Ed., *Computer Supported Collaborative Writing.* London: Springer-Verlag, 1993.
> [2] V. L. Zammuner, 'Individual and co-operative computer writing and revising: Who gets the best results?' *Learning and Instruction*, vol. 5, no.2, pp. 101–24, 1995.
> [3] C. Tang, 'Effects of collaborative learning on the quality of assignments,' in *Teaching and Learning in Higher Education*, B. Dart and G. Boulton-Lewis, Eds. Melbourne: Australian Council for Educational Research, 1998, pp. 102–23.
> [4] B. W. M. Speck, T. R. Johnson, C. P. Dice and L. B. Heaton, *Collaborative Writing: An Annotated Bibliography.* Westport, Connecticut: Greenwood Press, 1999.

An alternative version is to list (and number) the authors *alphabetically* in the reference list, and to assign these numbers to the authors in the text as appropriate.

4   The Vancouver style, popular in medical journals, is named after its inception following agreements made during a meeting in Vancouver in 1987 by the International Steering Committee of Medical Editors. Here, as with the IEEE system, the authors are numbered in the text in order of their appearance, and the numbers are enclosed in square brackets. The reference list is numbered sequentially, but the authors are listed surnames first, followed by their initials. Again the dates of publications are given after journal titles, or at the ends of the references for books etc. The key feature of the Vancouver style is its 'spare' typography and punctuation, and the use of abbreviated journal titles.

For example:

1   Sharples M, editor. Computer supported collaborative writing. London: Springer-Verlag, 1993.
2   Zammuner VL. Individual and co-operative computer writing and revising: Who gets the best results? Learn Instruc 1995;5 (Pt 2): 101–24.
3   Tang C. Effects of collaborative learning on the quality of assignments. In: Dart B, Boulton-Lewis G, editors. Teaching and learning in higher education. Melbourne: Australian Council for Educational Research, 1998;102–23.
4   Speck BWM, Johnson TR, Dice CP, Heaton LB. Collaborative writing: an annotated bibliography. Westport, CT: Greenwood Press, 1999.

Each of these main referencing systems has advantages and disadvantages for both readers and authors. Some key points are, first, that the name(date) system clutters the text when long lists of references are given. For example, twenty names and dates might be cited in a row, whereas in the numbered system one simply puts [1–20]. Incidentally there seems to be some confusion here in the name(date) system over whether or not these lists of names and dates should be cited in alphabetical or historical order. I recommend one or the other (but not a mixture, as sometimes is the case). Second, it is difficult for readers to judge the recency of an in-text reference in a numbered reference system. Third, in writing the text, getting all of the numbers in sequence is tedious, especially when revising or rewriting the text (if this is not computer-aided). Finally, abbreviated journal titles cause difficulty for readers and authors unfamiliar with the abbreviations.

REASONS FOR CITING REFERENCES

According to Robillard (2006), *students* are taught that 'the primary function of citing references is to avoid plagiarism by giving credit where credit is due'. However, when it comes to publishing academic papers, the reasons for citing references increase. Robillard suggests that references:

- tell the readers where they can find the material being discussed;
- provide evidence for the writers' claims;
- draw the readers' attention to little-known or unknown work;
- indicate to the reader the scholarship of the writer:
  (a) by displaying erudition, and
  (b) through self-citation;
- show the writers' respect for particular people;
- align the author with particular schools of thought; and
- allow mutual grooming: colleagues cite colleagues and friends, and vice versa.

Indeed, there is a small research literature on the benefits or otherwise of making self-citations (e.g. see Fowler and Aksnes, 2007; Hellsten *et al.*, 2007). Fowler and Aksnes report (in a study of more than half a million citations made by Norwegian scientists) that the more one cites oneself, the more one is cited by others.

CITING PAGE NUMBERS FOR QUOTATIONS IN THE TEXT

There is some debate in the literature about the necessity for citing in the text the page numbers of a quotation, table or figure from another article when giving a reference to it. Generally speaking, this is done more frequently in papers in the arts than it is in the sciences, and studies have shown that many science journals are lax in this respect (e.g. Donovan, 2006; Henige, 2006). Clearly the level of detail required for an in-text reference is a matter of debate, but the actual page numbers can be very helpful for readers if they want to check up on what was actually said or shown.

Sometimes it is not possible for writers to include the page numbers of a specific quotation because they are working from a prepublication electronic text and it is simpler to refer the reader to the final printed publication than to the unique resource location (URL) for the preliminary or alternative version. (This explains why there is no page number for the quotation from Robillard cited above!) Nevertheless, the moral of the tale, however tedious, is that it is best to include information rather than leave it out. Someone, somewhere, will want to check it.

USING APPROPRIATE STYLES AND REFERENCES

In most situations authors have no say in what reference system will be used, and they prepare their texts in accordance with publishers' demands. They do, however, have different aims and can use different referencing styles to match these, as shown in Table 2.10.1.

Historical analysis shows that referencing styles are not fixed and predetermined, and that incoming editors can and do make changes. *The British Journal of Psychology*, for example, started in 1910 with a footnote system and continued this until 1930. Between 1930 and 1950, a variety of systems were used within individual volumes: in 1930, for example, Volume 21 had mainly footnotes, but one article included a bibliography. In 1940, it was possible to find articles in the same volume:

(i)   with footnotes;
(ii) with a numbered reference system and a sequential listing of the references; and
(iii) with an alphabetical listing of the references in a numbered sequence.

In 1953, the journal changed to the current name(date) system of referencing.

In other journals, such changes have been more abrupt. *The American Journal of Psychology*, for instance, used footnotes from 1887 until 1970 and then it changed to the name(date) system in 1971. *The American Psychologist* started life in 1946 with a numbered referencing system and an alphabetical listing of the references until it changed to the name(date) system in 1959. Connors (1999) cites similar changes in other APA and MLA journals, concluding that, ' the APA style now bids fair to become the de facto standard for all fields over the next five decades' (p. 232). Connors' judgement now seems premature.

Table 2.10.1 Writers' aims and preferred referencing styles

Aim	Style
To communicate to fellow colleagues/scholars	Style of own discipline
To communicate to a different (academic) audience	Style of that discipline
To communicate to a general academic audience	Style of journal chosen
To communicate to students within own discipline	Style of own discipline
To communicate to students generally	Few references needed
To communicate to the general public	No formal references needed

Reproduced from Hartley (2002) by permission of Sage Publications Ltd.

REFERENCES

Connors, R. J. (1999). The rhetoric of citation systems – Part II: Competing epistemic values in citation. *Rhetoric Review*, *17*(2), 219–36.

Donovan, S. K. (2006). Comment: Discouraging verification: Citation practices across disciplines. *Journal of Scholarly Publication*, *37*(4), 313–16.

EndNote (2007). EndNote information. Retrieved 19 May 2007 from www.endnote.com/eninfo.asp.

Fowler, J. H. & Aksnes, D. W. (2007). Does self-citation pay? *Scientometrics*, *72*(3), 427–47.

Hartley, J. (2002). On choosing typographic settings for reference lists. *Social Studies of Science*, *32*(5–6), 917–32.

Hellsten, T., Lambiotte, R., Scharnhorst, A. & Ausloos, M. (2007). Self-citations, co-authorships and keywords: A new approach to scientists' field mobility? *Scientometrics*, *72*(3), 469–86.

Henige, D. (2006). Discouraging verification: Citation practices across the disciplines. *Journal of Scholarly Publication*, *37*(2), 99–118.

Robillard, A. E. (2006). Young scholars affecting composition: A challenge to disciplinary citation practice. *College English*, *68*(3), 253–70.

FURTHER READING

Hutson, S. R. (2006). Self-citation in Archaeology: Age, gender, prestige, and the self. Retrieved 20 January 2007 from *Journal of Archaeological Methods and Theory*, *13*(1) (page numbers unspecified) (www.ingentaconnect.com/content/klu/jarm).

Footnotes

Some journals in some disciplines use footnotes as well as references. Footnotes are most commonly found in journals in the humanities and least in journals in the sciences, with social science journals somewhere in between. Footnotes serve the same purposes as references, as outlined by Robillard in the previous chapter (p. 60) perhaps more clearly. The differences are that they are sometimes more extensive than references, often containing more exposition, and they usually appear, as their name suggests, at the foot of the page. However, it is also common to find such notes at the end of a chapter, or even grouped chapter by chapter at the end of a book.

The use of footnotes has an ancient pedigree. Slomanson (1987) dates the first use of the term to 1822, but cites the use of footnotes occurring shortly after 1066. Grafton (1997) is more cautious. He writes, 'Scholars have placed the birth of the footnote in the twelfth century, the seventeenth, the eighteenth, and the nineteenth – never without good reason' (p. viii). Be that as it may, what appears to happen with many academic journals is that footnotes first appear in their early history, but that these are then replaced with numbered references, before finally a name(date) system takes over (as described in the previous chapter).

The literature on writers' and readers' attitudes to footnotes is long on anecdote and assertion, but short on evidence (Hartley, 1999). Two common assertions are:

(i) that footnotes seem irresistible, and that they can thus distract the reader;[1] and
(ii) that it is sometimes difficult to find your place back in the main text to continue reading when you have moved away to read the footnote.

In order to obtain some data on feelings such as these, I once gave a questionnaire on the topic to approximately fifty academics whose disciplinary

---

1   See what I mean . . .

journals typically used footnotes (e.g. law, history, education and English and modern languages), and to another fifty whose disciplinary journals typically did not (e.g. medicine, physics and psychology). The questionnaire asked these academics about:

1   their attitudes to footnotes generally;
2   their attitudes to footnotes being placed at the ends of individual chapters as opposed to the end of a book; and
3   their preferences for notes or references being placed at the ends of individual chapters in a book rather than at the end of the book (or vice versa) when the chapters were written:
    (a) by the same author, or
    (b) by different authors.

The results showed that both groups of academics responded positively to footnotes – that is, they did not find them irritating. However, as might be anticipated, the members of the 'footnotes' group were significantly more positive towards footnotes than were the members of the 'no-footnotes' group. The 'footnotes' group claimed that they had significantly less difficulty in returning to where they were on the page after reading a footnote, and that footnotes could be less easily ignored than did the 'no-footnotes' group.

However, the respondents in both groups agreed that:

1   notes at the ends of chapters or books were more irritating than notes at the foot of the page;
2   it was difficult to find your way back to where you originally were after reading a note at the end of a chapter or a book, as opposed to a note at the foot of the page; and
3   it was better to have notes or references at the end of each chapter (as here) rather than at the end of the book, especially when the chapters were written by different authors.

These findings suggest that readers attach greater significance to the value of footnotes and endnotes if they are used to reading them in their books and journals. They thus form an accepted way of conveying additional information within certain disciplines. However, for a more general audience, it might be best to avoid them.[2]

2   Caught you again?

REFERENCES

Grafton, A. (1997). *The footnote: A curious history.* Cambridge, MA: Harvard University Press.

Hartley, J. (1999). What do we know about footnotes? Opinions and data. *Journal of Information Science*, 25(3), 205–12.

Slomanson, W. R. (1987). The bottom line: Footnote logic in law review writing. *Legal References Services Quarterly*, 7(1), 47–69.

FURTHER READING

Bensman, J. (1988). The aesthetics and politics of footnoting. *Politics, Culture and Society*, 1(3), 443–70.

Jansen, F., van Lijf, A. & Toussaint, E. (2002). A note on the evaluation of footnotes and other devices for background information in popular scientific texts. *IEEE Transactions on Professional Communication*, 44(3), 195–201.

Stiff, P. (1997). 'A footnote kicks him': How books make readers work. *Journal of Scholarly Publishing*, 28(2), 65–75.

Responding to referees

As noted in the postscript to Chapter 1.1, refereeing can be a lottery. Referees' comments – and recommendations – can vary. Consider three more referees' advice and comments to an editor about an article that I had submitted for publication:

- *Referee 1*: Accept. It would be quite helpful to non-specialists to provide grade reading equivalents to the Flesch scores to give perspective.
- *Referee 2*: Accept with revision. This paper addresses an interesting and important topic . . . Despite this . . . the results are somewhat of a mixed bag overall. Accordingly I would recommend the following revisions before it is considered for publication. I begin with the more serious concerns and then touch on some relatively minor ones . . .
- *Referee 3*: Reject. [. . .] This paper conflates (this technical task) with some non-technical terms, some common-sense beliefs about reading and writing that there is no strong evidence for, normative expectations of what texts should be and moralistic stances towards textual patterns, and relies unanalytically on a measure that aggregates factors and itself is not widely respected . . .

These quotations are extracts from the referees' reports. Which referee do you imagine I found most useful when asked by the editor to consider them all when making a resubmission? Answer: Referee 2. Referee 1 was complimentary, but did not require much. The report contained only three sentences and was rather cursory. Referee 2 wrote two pages of useful suggestions and I was able to use most of these to improve the paper. Referee 3 wrote at length but required a completely different approach to the topic so that there was not much I could do to meet these criticisms.

There are similar accounts in the literature of irreconcilable comments from referees (e.g. see Griffiths, 1992). So what do you do, especially if you get a rejection letter? Here is one suggestion:

> When you are the recipient of an unexpected rejection letter, don't sit down and fire off a letter to the editor. Talk it over with your friends. Indulge in intemperate verbal expressions to your colleagues. Write a letter to the editor that says exactly what you want to say, then delete it . . .
>
> (Warren, 2000, p. 172)

The first thing is to calm down. It may take a week or two, but eventually you may begin to see that what the referees say might have some sense. Then you can start to revise your manuscript.

It is probably wiser to revise the manuscript than just send it without changes to another journal. Different journals have different requirements, and it is important to try to meet these, as well as to pre-empt the criticisms made by the original referees (Donovan, 2007).

If you are luckier and an editor asks you 'to revise and resubmit' you can take the opportunity to improve your paper. Most editors ask you to indicate when you resubmit your manuscript what you have done to meet the criticisms of the referees. Figure 2.12.1 shows a typical reply for another paper. Here it can be seen that the main focus of Referee 2's comments (that the article was not theoretical enough) has been skirted round, but that most of the less important criticisms have been taken on board. In this case the editor accepted the revised manuscript for publication, indicating that she found the reply to be 'a balanced and constructive response'.

Woods (1999) suggests that authors keep working on their papers once they have been submitted, especially if they come across some new and relevant findings that ought to be included or discussed. This is sensible advice, as this will help authors to respond more authoritatively to any referees' criticisms when they eventually arrive.

Summary of changes made in revising an article

Re – referee 1

A summary has been added to meet this reviewer's suggestion.

Re – referee 2

General comments

This referee finds the paper descriptive and a-theoretical, and wants a different approach. We have not met this requirement – largely because it would involve completely re-writing the paper from a different viewpoint. We have, however, met this criticism in places by responding to it. Thus we have moved up Panel 1 from the end of the Introduction to the beginning of the paper, and we have explicitly said (pp. 7–8) that we are not particularly interested in a theoretical approach at this stage. Indeed, Panel 1 implicitly lists 20 theories – so there is no consensus anyway.

Specific changes

We have given the proportion of the sample who were Mature students in the abstract, as requested.

We have added a paragraph to explain the rationale for including the analyses of the sub-sample as well as the main one (p. 10).

We have clarified the description of the results on p. 10 (originally) and on p. 12 (originally) as requested.

We have deleted Table 5 and the discussion around it as suggested.

We have explained more clearly the rationale for choosing the two methods of standardisation (now on p. 16).

We have not commented on why the results differ for the different methods of assessment – as we do not feel this is necessary.

We have taken the opportunity in doing the revisions to:
- Add more relevant references where appropriate.
- To re-write the sub-section in the introduction on small-scale studies of sex differences under three sub-headings to match the previous text. (In doing this we found a set of results on essay examinations had not been included in the original submission!)

Figure 2.12.1 The authors' response to an editorial request to consider the comments of two referees in revising a manuscript.

REFERENCES

Donovan, S. K. (2007). The importance of resubmitting rejected papers. *Journal of Scholarly Publishing*, *38*(3), 151–5.

Griffiths, M. (1992). Under (peer) pressure. *The Psychologist*, *5*(7), p. 336.

Warren, M. G. (2000). Reading reviews, suffering rejection, and advocating for your paper. In R. J. Sternberg (Ed.), *Guide to publishing in psychology journals* (pp. 169–86). Cambridge: Cambridge University Press.

Woods, P. (1999). *Successful writing for qualitative researchers*. London: Routledge.

FURTHER READING

Gosden, H. (2003). 'Why not give us the full story?': Functions of referees' comments in peer reviews of scientific research papers. *Journal of English for Academic Purposes*, *2*(2), 87–101.

Wagner, R. K. (2000). Rewriting the psychology paper. In R. J. Sternberg (Ed.). *Guide to publishing in psychology journals* (pp. 187–96). Cambridge: Cambridge University Press.

Proofs

The day will come when the proofs of an article that you submitted some months ago arrive unexpectedly in the post or on your screen. The proofs will be accompanied by a note:

1 indicating that they need to be corrected and returned to the publishers within a day or two; and
2 making dire threats about the costs of making major changes.

Proofs allow the author to check the accuracy of the typesetting, especially if the text has been altered to fit the printer's house style, and possibly to make minor changes. In point of fact, most proofs these days have few spelling and typographical errors because the text is handled electronically. However, errors still creep in. It is indeed amazing that these 'typos' do occur, despite the fact that the text has been repeatedly read by the author(s), the journal editor, the referees and the copy editor setting the text.

Checking the accuracy of the typesetting is not the same as reading the text. When reading we make inferences, and the text flows on without us noticing minor errors. When checking the proofs, we need to look at every word, every number and every comma separately, two or three times at least. Some authors find it useful to read the individual sentences and the table entries backwards, and to do it at least twice – on separate occasions – using fresh copies of the text each time.

Publishers using printed rather than electronic methods usually supply a set of 'proofreaders' marks' – ways of indicating changes – that they send to the authors with the proofs (see Day and Gastel, 2006, p. 134). Authors are required to mark the text and to indicate in the margins their requirements. However, these days, electronic proofs are more common, and these are typically accompanied by a numbered set of 'author queries'. Here, the numbers are printed in the text at the appropriate places, and a numbered list of queries is printed at the end. Typically, these ask about minor things, such as the spelling of a particular word or name; page numbers omitted in a reference; the date of a reference in the text being different from that in the reference list; the name of an author in the text spelled differently in the reference list; and whether or not references listed as 'in press' when the manuscript was submitted can now be updated, and so on.

These queries apply to the proofs as they are printed. Making changes rather than corrections is more complicated. Minor revisions of grammar may be acceptable, but complete revisions of paragraphs of text, deletions and insertions are not. Including a new additional reference might be appropriate if the name(date) system is used, but it might be seen as more difficult if a numbering system is used and every subsequent reference number has to be changed in both the text and the reference list. Making changes can thus be time-consuming and expensive if the results require re-pagination of the article and, indeed, possibly the whole issue of the journal in question.

Nonetheless, electronic typesetting makes this much easier than it was. Consequently, I find it helpful when returning proofs to indicate those changes that are essential, those that are optional, and those that might fit in between. For example, if the spacing between the elements in a table is poorly done, then you can ask for this to be improved, but, if you want to move a table (say back from the discussion to the results section where you originally placed it), then I find it best to ask if this can be done (Hartley, 2007). Often there is more space available to make changes than you think, as few articles run to the foot of their final page.

Sometimes, authors will find that a copy editor has changed what they originally wrote to make it fit the house style. Thus, a structured abstract might emerge in a traditional block form, a sentence written in a lively present tense might be rewritten in the passive, and your in-text boxed examples relabelled as appendices and placed at the end of the article. Authors need to reaffirm that what they wrote is what they want, and hope that it will be achieved.

REFERENCES

Day, R. A. & Gastel, B. (2006). *How to write and publish a scientific paper* (6th edn). Cambridge: Cambridge University Press.

Hartley, J. (2007). Guiding the copy editor: Positioning tables and figures in the text. *PsyPAG Quarterly Newsletter*, Issue 63, June, pp. 54–9.

Section 3

Other genres

Books

Books come in all shapes and sizes, and so do their purposes. Consequently it is difficult to offer specific advice in a text of this kind. We can, however, consider two general issues here:

(i) the relative difficulty of writing one kind of text over another; and
(ii) general procedures in publishing books.

DIFFERENT KINDS OF BOOKS

I list here some different kinds of book with my – probably biased – estimates of how time-consuming and difficult it is to write them.

1   The popular science book (e.g. texts such as those by Oliver Sacks, Carl Sagan, Stephen Jay Gould):
    These books are extremely easy to read, but they are probably much more difficult to write than it might seem. There might be much more polishing of the text than meets the eye. However it is done, it is beyond most of us.

2   The edited collection of previously published papers by the *same* author:
    These books can only be written by well-established authors who want to show their contribution to the field. These books may, or may not, be suitable for course texts.

3   The edited collection of previously published papers written by *different* authors:
    These books require much less writing by the editors, and the task is perhaps made more enjoyable if there are two or more of them who can share the debate about what to include. There is an opportunity here to include famous papers, but part of the art lies in avoiding large payments for copyright fees. These books sometimes form the basis for a course textbook. They may, or may not, suit all students on other similarly named courses in other institutions.

4   The edited collection of original chapters written by several different authors:
    These books take longer to produce – not all of the potential authors deliver their chapters on time. These books have the advantage, though, of being more up to date than books in 2 or 3 above, but their contents might not be so outstanding, or well-known.
5   The conference collection:
    Here many authors are often involved and consequently there is more room for delay. However, the conference collection (if it is not delayed in publication) can present the state of the art, particularly in new and developing fields.
6   The handbook:
    The handbook combines categories 4 and 5. Here, the book is usually larger and the multiple chapters are original ones (usually reviews), written by acknowledged experts in the field. The handbook usually has a long gestation period and wider coverage and is destined for the library shelves rather than the personal library.
7   The individually authored textbook:
    This is perhaps the most satisfying kind of book for an individual to write but it can be a hard slog. It is easier if you have a number of previous contributions to draw on.

GENERAL PROCEDURES

In order to publish a book, it is useful to think first about an appropriate publisher. Some publishers will have books on similar topics in their 'list', and others won't. It might be best to look to the first kind, for they will know the market better. Then it is a good idea to check these publishers out on the Web. Each will have a homepage with details about submissions – and possibly the names of their commissioning editors for the different categories of texts that they publish. A letter to such a person, making general enquiries about the suitability of what you propose to do, is then in order.

Many publishers have actual proposal forms on the Web. It is interesting to compare them, but they are fairly similar. What the publishers require is a synopsis of the text, probably one or two sample chapters and, sometimes, some indication of the author's prowess in the field. What they also require is an estimate of the 'competition' and of the size of the market: in other words, how many books will sell? For a proposal to succeed, the book 'needs to be of high quality, original, with no or few competitors, have a clearly defined audience, and promise to be a product (the publisher) can market at a reasonable price' (Woods, 1998, p. 129). Figure 3.1.1 shows an extract from the Web-based proposal form for Routledge – the publishers of this

Submitting a proposal

Four main areas need to be addressed:

1   A statement of aims including 3–4 paragraphs outlining the rationale behind the book:
    - Quite simply, what is your book about?
    - What are its main themes and objectives?
    - What are you doing differently, or in a more innovative way, or better than existing books?

2   A detailed synopsis and chapter headings with an indication of length and schedule:
    - Please list working chapter headings and provide a paragraph of explanation on what you intend to cover in each chapter.
    - This may be all that the reviewer has to go on, so a list of chapter headings alone is not enough.
    - If sample chapters, or a draft manuscript are available, please send them or let us know when they will be available.
    - How many tables, diagrams or illustrations will there be (roughly)?
    - Roughly how many thousand words in length will your book be?
    - Does this include references and footnotes? Most of our books are 80,000–100,000 words long.
    - When will you be able to deliver the completed typescript?
    - Please be as realistic as possible.

3   A description of the target market:
    - Who is your book primarily aimed at? Who will buy it? Who will read it?
    - Is it aimed at an undergraduate or postgraduate student audience?
    - What courses would the book be used on?
    - Is it a research monograph that will sell primarily to academic libraries?
    - Is the subject area of the proposal widely taught, or researched?
    - Would this subject have international appeal outside your home country? If so, where?

4   A list of the main competing books:
    - We would like some indication that you are familiar with competition to your proposed book. What are their strengths & weaknesses? What makes your book better then the existing competition?

It will also be necessary to include:

1   one or two sample chapters, or a draft manuscript, if available;
2   a curriculum vitae of all authors, and notes on any other contributors.

Figure 3.1.1 Extracts from Routledge's book proposal form.

Available at www.routledge.com; reproduced with permission of the publishers.

text. Examples of authors' actual proposals can be found in Haynes (2001, pp. 8–10 and 164–70) and Woods (1998, pp. 135–41).

If the commissioning editor likes the proposal, (s)he will take it to the relevant committee and, if they like it, the proposal is then (usually) sent out to referees. Sometimes authors are asked to nominate two or three such persons themselves, but not always. If the referees are favourable and make helpful suggestions, then the book might be deemed acceptable for publication – subject to a forthcoming contract.

Haynes (2001) considers the pros and cons of submitting a book proposal to one or more publishers at the same time. He comes to the conclusion that it is better to submit proposals to one publisher at a time as:

a) commissioning editors will be annoyed if they find out that you have sent the proposal to other publishers behind their backs; and
b) feedback from rejected proposals will help to improve the next submission.

Once you have got as far as the contract, you need to study it carefully – and perhaps discuss it with other authors that you know. There are things to look out for and to see if you can change – such as a low royalty rate – and there are things you might delete (such as guaranteeing that your next book will be considered first by this particular publisher). Other questions to ask include:

• Are royalties paid as a percentage of the list price (e.g. ten per cent of the cost of the book in a shop) or as a percentage of the publisher's net receipts (e.g. ten per cent of what the retailer returns to the publisher)? The latter will be less.
• Is the royalty rate increased after a given number of the books have been sold?
• If there is an advance against royalties, is this paid when you sign the contract, when you submit the manuscript or when the book appears?
• How many free copies of the book do you get?
• How long are you given to correct the proofs and to prepare the index?

Items such as these are negotiable.

Haynes (2006) contrasts 'authors from hell' with 'dream writers' in terms of their behaviours (see Table 3.1.1).

Finally, these days authors need to consider their electronic rights. Many publishers now publish electronic versions of their printed texts as they occur, and they want to control the electronic book rights. Such rights require careful consideration. Advice can be found in the Society of Authors' *Quick Guide 8: Publishing Contracts* (2003).

Table 3.1.1 Authors from hell versus dream writers

Authors from hell	Dream writers
• Behave as though their book is the only one the publisher is considering	• Read their contracts
• Believe their reputation is greater than it is	• Alert the publishers to any difficulties
• Believe their own marketing ideas are incontrovertibly good ones – regardless of reality, cost or time	• Are happy to negotiate their contracts
• Break their contracts serially	• Write on the right subject, at the right level to the right length by the specified date
• Are far too busy to contemplate collecting permissions or to create an index	

Adapted from Haynes (2006) with permission of the author and the Society of Authors. © Anthony Haynes.

WRITING THE BOOK

In writing a book, an author obviously wants to keep to the contract as far as possible but, by the very nature of things, may want to change some aspects of it. A chapter might get expanded, or deleted, or the sequence of the contents might change, and so on, but authors need to stick as far as possible to the underlying idea of the basic proposal. Some publishers send the final manuscript out to reviewers for further comments and adjustments before setting it for publication.

REFERENCES

Haynes, A. (2001). *Writing successful textbooks.* London: A. & C. Black.
Haynes, A. (2006). Authors from hell. *The Author*, CXVII(3), 99–100.
Society of Authors. (2003). *Quick Guide 8: Publishing contracts.* London: Society of Authors.
Woods, P. (1998). *Successful writing for qualitative researchers.* London: Routledge.

FURTHER READING

Luey, B. (2002). *Handbook for academic authors* (4th edn). Cambridge: Cambridge University Press.

Theses

I have on my desk a Dutch Ph.D. thesis (Kools, 2005). It is published, at the author's expense, in a paperback format, with a colourful, glossy cover, and it can be bought like an academic textbook. The content, in English, contains eight chapters together with an introduction and a summary. Seven of these eight chapters are basically reprints of academic papers, one of which has appeared in print, two of which are 'in press', and four of which have been submitted for publication. Other Dutch theses contain, with linking commentaries, only chapters that have been previously published or are 'in press' (e.g. Geraerts, 2006).

I mention this to make two points:

1   that the ways of writing theses differ in different countries; and
2   that it might be useful to think about subsequent publication when writing a thesis . . .

WRITING A THESIS

Writing a thesis is like writing an academic article, only worse. The thesis is much longer. Unfortunately, students normally write their thesis before they start on articles, and they only write one. Thus, thesis writers typically have less practice and are less skilled at academic writing than are the more experienced authors of papers. Furthermore, many Ph.D. students writing their theses in English are non-native speakers of the language.

> A thesis is much like a graduate student: It has a limited purpose and a small audience; it is often insecure and defensive, justifying itself with excessive documentation; it is too narrowly focussed; and it has not yet developed a style of its own.
>
> (Luey, 2002, p. 34)

Disciplinary differences

There are disciplinary differences in theses, as there are in articles, in how they are written. Parry (1998) examined twenty-four Australian theses, eight in the arts, eight in the social sciences, and eight in the sciences. She showed that the language of theses (like that of articles) varied subtly within different disciplines. Parry argued that students had to learn to master these subject variations without being taught them explicitly. She found that, in the arts theses, there was a strong emphasis on argument in the writing, with writers arguing for new perspectives on the phenomena they were discussing. Arts theses were thus highly personalised and subjective. In the social science theses, Parry also found a strong emphasis on argument, but the arguments here were more likely to be based upon using and creating evidence, often in order to change the status quo. Parry found less argument in the science theses. Here, a series of studies was often reported, leading to statements and conclusions based upon the findings.

Different kinds of thesis

Paltridge (2002) described, with examples, four types of thesis, based upon an analysis of fifteen master's and fifteen Australian Ph.D. theses. These types were:

1 *Traditional (simple)*: Here, typically, there were six sections: introduction, literature review, materials and methods, results, discussion and conclusions – the IMRAD structure writ large.
2 *Traditional (complex)*: Here there were more sections, for example introduction; background to the study and literature review; background theory and methods (optional); study 1 – IMRAD; study 2 – IMRAD, study 3 etc.; general discussion and conclusions.
3 *Topic-based*: This type of thesis typically began with an introductory chapter followed by a series of chapters that had titles based on the sub-topics of the main topic under investigation, for example introduction; topic 1; topic 2; topic 3, etc.; conclusions.
4 *Compilation theses*: These theses comprised a compilation of research articles (as in Kools and Geraerts), for example introduction; background; research article 1; research article 2; research article 3, etc.; discussion and conclusions.

To this list we can add a fifth type:

5 *The professional or practitioner doctorate*: Here, the chapters might be formed of pre-prints of articles targeted at practitioner journals, or a mixture of both theoretical and practitioner chapters. These theses are likely to be shorter and more practical than traditional theses.

Some people have discussed other, non-traditional forms of theses. Duke and Beck (1999), for instance, discuss the novel as a form of thesis, and presentations in CD-ROM format.

These different formats for different types of thesis affect the students' writing requirements. Thus, for example, the initial literature review is probably more detailed and complex in the traditional thesis than it is in the compilation one. Furthermore, the audiences are different. The chapters in compilation theses are reprints of material written for a more specific, targeted audience (the readership of the journal in which they were first published), whereas the traditional thesis is targeted at a wider audience and is, therefore, perhaps more difficult to write. Similarly, the conclusion sections of topic-based theses will be different from those of compilation or traditional theses.

ELECTRONIC THESES

It is now conventional for Ph.D. writers to use word processing facilities to write their texts. In addition, it is getting more common to produce an electronic version of the thesis. Apparently, more than 50,000 doctoral theses and 100,000 master's theses are produced annually in this way in the USA (Moxley, 2003). Some universities are progressing in this direction in the UK, although there is much debate over the necessary regulations. Currently, there is discussion about providing an electronic theses online service (EThOS) to replace (or add to) the present-day inter-library loan service (see www.ethos.ac.uk).

Most of the electronic theses that can be downloaded from the Web follow the conventional format of traditionally printed ones, but there are variations. Thus, some use colour, animation, sound and hypertext (which allows the readers to read them in any sequence they wish). Dorwick (2003) presents a case-history of the difficulties of creating a web-based hypertext as a Ph.D. thesis: his paper suggests that people have to be very determined to write a thesis in this manner.

There are clear benefits to writing an electronic thesis. Single copies of traditionally printed theses sit on the library shelves in single institutions and are rarely read. Electronic theses are more easily available, making the contents accessible to a wider range of readers.

STRATEGIES FOR THE BEGINNING THESIS WRITER

The following tips (updated from Hartley, 1997) may be helpful when starting to write a thesis:

- Try to be well organised. Plan well ahead. Try to keep to the plan.
- Examine two or three theses in your discipline/area. This will show you what is required and how best to present it. Consider how appendices can be used to include material that gets in the way of the flow of the argument.
- Write from the beginning. Do not leave 'writing up' until the end – you will forget what you did, and why you did it. So keep a written record. With word-processors you can easily add, change, move around or delete words, sentences, paragraphs and chapters. If the thesis is experimental, then early experiments and pilot studies should be written up in full at the time of doing them, even if this detail is not needed in the end.
- Make and keep clearly labelled back-up disks. Losing your work is shattering.
- Discuss what you are doing and why you are doing it with fellow students all the time. Report back to them on progress. Share methods, results and conclusions. Explaining things to others helps with the writing process.
- Think of how you might publish each chapter or parts of the thesis separately after the thesis is completed. Write them in such a way that it will be relatively easy to do this. Do not get distracted by this, however: the thesis comes first.
- Master at the outset the appropriate procedures for presenting text in your discipline, particularly the presentation of footnotes and references. References should be stored – preferably on a database – from the outset, in full detail. There is nothing worse than trying to find again something that you read several months ago, just to record the part number or the page numbers.
- Read the requirements of your institution for the presentation of the thesis. Most institutions, for instance, require the text to be double-spaced, and they specify the width of the margins necessary for binding the thesis. If you prepare your drafts to this specification, you will find that you will not make mistakes – such as producing tabular arrays that do not fit in. Also, remember that a larger type-size (say 12-point) with 1.5 line spacing is necessary on an A4 page to make the text more readable.
- Submit regular drafts of subsections of your thesis to your supervisor, and ask for guidance on your writing – particularly if you are an overseas student.
- Make sure your supervisor eventually sees the thesis as a whole. It is not possible to judge the thesis as a whole by reading subsections on their own.

DISSEMINATING THE RESULTS OF DOCTORAL RESEARCH

New technology encourages the dissemination of doctoral research. However, theses are not normally written in a style that is appropriate for dissemination in conferences, journals or textbooks. As Luey (1990) points out, 'Textbooks differ in the level of difficulty, in format, and in the degree of illustrations . . .' (p. 121) as well as in their audiences. The same is true of articles. Many of the chapters in this text-book are based upon previously published articles. Some of these were written for postgraduates, some for academics in general and some for specialists. But, in writing this text, I have had to rewrite them all to make them more suitable for a mixed audience.

Dinham and Scott (2001) reported on the percentages of graduate students carrying out certain activities to disseminate the findings of their theses. In their first study, there were 139 respondents. Sixty of these (forty-three per cent) had disseminated their findings in one or more ways: fifty-one had made conference presentations, fifty had published a journal article, nine had written book chapters, seven had written books, five had written 'dissertation abstracts', and two had published in newsletters and electronically.

In their second study, there were fifty-three respondents. Here thirty-three (sixty-two per cent) had published the results of their research in some form before graduation, and forty-one (seventy-seven per cent) since graduation. Students who were supported by their supervisors and/or institutional policies had a significantly higher rate of publication that did those who were not.

REFERENCES

Dinham, S. & Scott, C. (2001). The experience of disseminating the results of doctoral research. *Journal of Further and Higher Education*, 25(1), 45–55.

Dorwick, K. (2003). Weeping stones, living trees: Creating and archiving electronic texts in student and scholarly writing. In J. R. Walker & O. O. Oviedo (Eds). *TnT: Texts and technology* (pp. 113–35). Cresskill, NJ: Hampton Press.

Duke, N. K. & Beck, S. W. (1999). Education should consider alternative formats for the dissertation. *Educational Researcher*, 28(3), 31–6.

Geraerts, E. (2006). *Remembrance of things past: The cognitive psychology of remembering and forgetting trauma*. Maastricht, NL: Maastricht University Press.

Hartley, J. (1997). Writing the thesis. In N. Graves & V. Varma (Eds.), *Working for a doctorate; A guide for the humanities and social sciences* (pp. 96–112). London: Routledge.

Kools, M. (2005). *Get the picture? A cognitive-psychological approach to systematic health education materials design*. Maastricht, NL: Maastricht University Press.

Luey, B. (2002). *Handbook for academic authors* (4th edn). Cambridge: Cambridge University Press.

Moxley, J. M. (2003). The role of compositionists in creating the networked digital library of theses and dissertations. In J. R. Walker & O. O. Oviedo (Eds.), *TnT: Texts and technology* (pp. 137–47). Cresskill, NJ: Hampton Press.

Paltridge, B. (2002). Thesis and dissertation writing: An examination of published advice and actual practice. *English for Specific Purposes*, *21*(2), 125–43.

Parry, S. (1998). Disciplinary differences in doctoral theses. *Higher Education*, *36*, 273–99.

FURTHER READING

Kamler, B. & Thomson, P. (2006). *Helping doctoral students write: Pedagogies for supervision.* Abingdon: Routledge.

Murray, R. (2006). *How to write a thesis* (2nd edn). Maidenhead: Open University Press.

Pollard, R. Q. (2005). From dissertation to journal article: A useful method for planning and writing any manuscript. *The Internet Journal of Mental Health*, *2*(2) (pages unspecified) (www.ispub.com/ostia/index.php).

Literature reviews

Whether it be a thesis or a paper, it is normal practice to begin with a literature review. The aims of these reviews can vary, however, and how they are tackled depends upon their purpose. Literature reviews can:

- show the history of a field;
- review the work done in a specific time period – for example 'The annual review of . . .';
- plot the development of a line of reasoning;
- integrate and synthesise work from different research areas;
- evaluate the current state of evidence for a particular viewpoint;
- reveal inadequacies in the literature and point to where further research needs to be done.

These different purposes define and control how and where writers search for the relevant information to review. Typically, researchers start by following up the references provided in several key papers and then proceed to the Internet (see Fink, 2005). The accumulating information (it never ceases) can be filed – electronically or in paper-based folders (see Chapter 4.1). If it is appropriate, it is also helpful at this stage to email or write to the authors of original papers to obtain copies of the materials used in experimental studies for, in my experience, the brief descriptions of such materials in journal articles do not do them justice.

STRATEGIES FOR PRESENTING RESULTS IN REVIEWS

There are at least six ways of presenting summaries of the results of research reviews, which can be placed along a continuum of statistical precision.

1   *The narrative review*: This is the kind of review that is typically used in this book. Writers research around a particular topic and then write a

review of the field, giving their own 'take' on it, selecting evidence from whatever seems appropriate to them. This type of review is most common in text-books and popular journals. I once provided a case-history account of how to write such a review that was motivated by the need to rebut a claim by the UK government that primary school children benefited from doing homework (Hartley, 2000). The government had used spurious claims in order to specify how many hours each week children in primary school should spend on homework.

2   *The narrative review with scoreboard*: Here, writers strengthen the arguments of their reviews by supporting the claims made with tabular 'scoreboards'. Table 3.3.1 shows an example (with fictitious data).

3   *A scoreboard plus details*: Table 3.3.2 shows an example (with limited data) of how more detail can be provided in a scoreboard. The advantages of listing individual studies in different categories are that it enables the reader to trace the studies should they wish and, if they are familiar with the field, to see if any have been omitted.

Table 3.3.1 A 'scoreboard' giving the number of studies that show homework has an effect at different ages[*]

| | No. of studies showing that homework has or does not have an effect | |
	Yes	No
Primary school studies	1	6
Secondary school studies	10	3

* Fictitious data.

Table 3.3.2 An extract from a more detailed (unpublished) 'scoreboard'[*]

| | Studies showing that homework has an effect | |
	Yes	No
Primary school	Alton-Lee and Nuthall (1990)	Cooper et al. (1998) Levin (1997) Miller et al. (1993)
Secondary school	Cooper et al. (1998) Holmes and Croll (1989) Keith and Benson (1992) Rutter et al. (1979) Tymms and FitzGibbon (1992) Zellman and Waterman (1999)	Faulkner and Blyth (1998) Mau (1997) Wharton (1997)

* With many references left out to save space.

4 A 'scoreboard' showing critical features: A common method of summarising results, particularly used in theses and dissertations, is to provide a table listing the key features of the studies being discussed. Table 3.3.3 provides a simplified and fictitious example. Such tables take a good deal of time to construct, but they can be enormously helpful for readers. The information provided in such tables also means that key information (e.g. the numbers and the ages of the participants, and the place of study) is not omitted, as often occurs in narrative reviews. Indeed, a series of such tables can be presented, each dealing with one particular feature in turn.

5 Meta-analytic 'scoreboards': Meta-analysis involves pooling the results that can be found from all the known studies on a given topic. Sometimes this number of studies is very high (e.g. studies of the effects of television), and sometimes it is quite small (e.g. studies of the effects of homework). The aim, however, is to arrive at an overall summary of the results for the topic in question.

To conduct a meta-analysis, all of the studies known to the researcher (or team of researchers) are accumulated, and the results are averaged according to certain rules. This usually involves, first of all, discarding a number of studies that do not include sufficient data, or the right kind of data (see below). Then, for each one of the remaining studies, the mean score of the control group is subtracted from the mean score of the experimental group, and the result is divided by the standard deviation of the control group (or both groups combined). Finally, the results obtained in step two are averaged over all the studies. The ensuing result is expressed in terms of an 'effect size' that indicates the importance of a particular variable. Table 3.3.4 provides an example from the field of homework. Effect sizes are typically interpreted as follows: 0.0 = no effect; 0.2 = small effect; 0.5 = medium effect; 0.8 = large effect. Thus, in Table 3.3.4, the effects of homework get larger as the children get older.

Table 3.3.3 A 'scoreboard' with critical features[*]

Study	Age group	Number of pupils	Subject matter	Length of study
Abba (1988)	5–7 yrs	20 per year	Arithmetic	1 week
Becca (1997)	7–8 yrs	2,0000	Varied	3 months
Cedda (2001)	6 yrs	10	Reading	7 weeks
Deffa (1999)	11–12 yrs	25 per year	English Maths	8 weeks
Egga (1996)	12–14 yrs	13 per year	Science	1 week
Fehha (2005)	15–16 yrs	21 per year	English Maths Science	8 weeks

[*] Fictitious data.

Table 3.3.4 Effect sizes for studies of the effectiveness of homework

	Homework versus no homework	Homework versus supervised study	Time spent on homework
Primary school	0.15	0.8	0.04
11–14 years	0.31	0.24	0.14
15–17 years	0.64	0.33	0.53

Adapted with permission from Cooper and Valentine (2001). © Taylor & Francis, www.informaworld. com.

Some people think that such meta-analytic reviews are superior to narrative reviews, but others provide criticisms (see Fink, 2005). To carry out a meta-analysis you need to know the sample sizes and the means and standard deviations of the experimental and control groups in every study included. This stricture, of course, excludes qualitative studies, and these studies can make important contributions. Student performance in homework is undoubtedly related to what they and their parents think about it. There is also some debate over whether or not some studies should be excluded from the averaging procedure – say on the grounds of limited sample sizes – but with meta-analytic studies it is usual to include all of the studies that one can. Some studies, however, do compare the results obtained with different procedures. Anderson's (2004) meta-analytic review of the effects of violent video games, for example, contrasted the results obtained when all of the studies known to the author were included with those obtained from a smaller sample of better studies. In this case the better studies yielded higher effect sizes.

6   *Evidence-based 'scoreboards'*: With the 'evidence-based' approach, more studies are excluded on particular methodological grounds when making the overall summary of the results. In medical research, for example, it is usual to exclude comparison studies where the participants have not been allocated at random into experimental and control conditions. However, it is difficult to do this in all areas of study, and randomised controlled trials (RCTs) are rare in social science research. Torgerson *et al.* (2003), for example, were only able to find twelve RCTs in 4,555 reported investigations into improving adult literacy and/or numeracy, and, I know of no RCTs on the topic of homework.

The criteria for including studies in evidence-based studies have thus got wider for disciplines in the social sciences compared with medicine, but there are still many strictures concerning what should and should not be included in reviews of this kind (see Andrews, 2005). The importance of the evidence-based approach becomes more obvious when the overall picture obtained from RCTs is different from that obtained from studies using other, less stringent methods. Guyatt *et al.* (2000), for example, found that the pooled results from ten studies using RCTs in the field of sex education for adolescents showed no significant effects for the treatments overall, whereas the pooled results from seventeen non-RCT studies showed the treatments to be effective . . .

SOME PROBLEMS

There are a number of problems in reviewing the literature that apply to all of the above strategies. First of all, there is what is sometimes called the 'file-drawer' problem. This relates to the fact that it is easier to publish studies that have statistically significant findings than it is to publish ones that do not, and so the latter get filed away. Torgerson (2006) calls this 'the Achilles heel' of systematic reviews, but it applies to all attempts to review the literature in any field.

Next, there is the problem of interpreting the findings of the published studies and seeing if these findings are relevant to your review. Research papers summarise a great deal of time and effort in a few pages. Reviewers summarise these papers in a few lines. Different reviewers emphasise different aspects of the same studies, and thus their accounts vary. Hartley (2000, pp. 166–7), for example, cites four different accounts of one particular study on homework. Readers reading only one of these may be mislead.

Relatedly, it may be more difficult to summarise adequately the results of qualitative studies. Dixon-Woods *et al.* (2006) discuss this at length in the context of summarising evidence-based studies and come to the conclusion that this really is a tricky problem.

Finally, there are some other assumptions made in literature reviews that do not withstand close scrutiny. These are:

1   that different dependent variables (manipulated by different investigators in different studies but designed to test the same hypotheses) are of equal validity or importance;
2   that the results obtained in one culture (e.g. American) are directly relevant to another one (e.g. British) and can thus be pooled together;
3   that the results obtained in one period (e.g. the 1960s) are the same as those that would be obtained today;
4   that the results obtained from limited samples (e.g. schoolchildren) apply to wider populations (e.g. adults); and
5   that the results obtained in simplified experiments apply to the much more complex 'real world'.

When writing a literature review, one solution to some of these problems is to examine in more detail the original papers and, in particular, the original materials used in the papers being reviewed. There are few examples of reviewers using such strategies – although it is clearly advisable to do so when writing the literature review in theses. Hartley *et al*. (1980) provided three such illustrations. One, by Macdonald-Ross (1977), concluded that Vernon's (1946) results on the effectiveness of diagrams arose largely as a consequence of her using poorly designed diagrams. Similarly, Elashoff and Snow (1971) were able to write a devastating critique of *Pygmalion in the Classroom* after examining the tests and procedures used by Rosenthal and Jacobson (1968). And finally, Klare (1976) read thirty-six studies on the effects of readability upon the comprehension of text. Nine of these were published papers, and twenty-seven were unpublished theses. Klare found that 100 per cent of the published studies contained statistically significant findings, compared with sixty per cent of the dissertations. This, of course, altered the nature of his review, and his conclusions.

REFERENCES

Anderson, C. A. (2004). An update on the effects of playing violent video games. *Journal of Adolescence*, 27(1), 113–22.

Andrews, R. (2005). The place of systematic reviews in educational research. *British Journal of Educational Studies*, 53(4), 399–416.

Cooper, H. & Valentine, J. C. (2001). Using research to answer practical questions about homework. *Educational Psychologist*, 36(3), 143–54.

Dixon-Woods, M., Bonas, S., Booth, A., Jones, D. R., Miller, T., Sutton, A. J., Shaw, R. L., Smith, J. A. & Young, B. (2006). How can systematic reviews incorporate qualitative research? A critical perspective. *Qualitative Research*, 6(1), 27–44.

Elashoff, J. D. & Snow, R. E. (1971). *Pygmalion reconsidered.* Worthington, OH: Charles A. Jones.

Fink, A. (2005). *Conducting research literature reviews: From Internet to paper.* Thousand Oaks, CA: Sage.

Guyatt, G., DiCenso, A., Farewell, V., Willan, A. & Griffith, L. (2000). Randomized trials versus observational studies in adolescent pregnancy prevention. *Journal of Clinical Epidemiology*, 53(2), 167–74.

Hartley, J. (2000). Investigating homework: An outsider's view. In J. Hartley & A. Branthwaite (Eds.), *The Applied Psychologist* (2nd edn, pp. 163–78). Buckingham: Open University Press.

Hartley, J., Branthwaite, A. & Cook, A. (1980). Writing reviews: Some problems of reviewing research in the social sciences. In J. Hartley (Ed.), *The psychology of written communication* (pp. 252–62). London: Kogan Page.

Klare, G. R. (1976). A second look at the validity of readability formulas. *Journal of Reading Behavior*, VIII(2), 129–52.

Macdonald-Ross, M. (1977). How numbers are shown: A review of the research on the presentation of quantitative information. *Audio-Visual Communication Review*, (25)4, 359–409.

Rosenthal, R. & Jacobson, L. (1968). *Pygmalion in the classroom.* New York: Holt, Rinehart & Winston.

Torgerson C. J. (2006). Publication bias: The Achilles heel of systematic reviews? *British Journal of Educational Studies*, 54(1), 89–102.

Torgerson, C. J., Porthouse, J. & Brooks, G. (2003). A systematic review and meta-analysis of randomised controlled trials evaluating interventions in adult literacy and numeracy. *Journal of Research in Reading*, 26(2), 234–55.

Vernon, M. D. (1946). Learning from graphical material. *British Journal of Psychology*, 36, 145–59.

FURTHER READING

Fink, A. (2005). *Conducting research literature reviews: From Internet to paper*. Thousand Oaks, CA: Sage.

Hart, C. (1998). *Doing a literature review*. Buckingham: Open University Press.

Kamler, B. & Thompson, P. (2006). *Helping doctoral students write: Pedagogies for supervision*. Abingdon: Routledge.

Petticrew, M. & Roberts, H. (2006). *Systematic reviews in the social sciences: A practical guide*. Oxford: Blackwell.

Conference papers

The conference paper has been described as 'the essential launching pad for nearly all scholarly careers' (Gould, 1995, p. 37). According to Drott (1995), nearly half of the conference papers published in the sciences and the social sciences in the 1960s went on to become published papers – usually within two years or so. Similar results were reported in the field of medicine (see Weller, 2002). However, others have reported smaller proportions than this. Drott (1995), for example, found that only thirteen per cent of conference papers in information science were developed into publications, and Stolk *et al.* (2002) report that only thirty per cent of conference papers in medical contexts found themselves in print. More recently, conference papers can be found as preprints in some databases, and Schwartz and Kennicutt (2004) report that such papers were cited twice as frequently as those not posted.

There is also some evidence, but not a lot, that presenting papers in seminars and conferences can lead to shorter refereeing times and greater success in the refereeing process. Hartley (2005), for instance, found shorter refereeing times for papers previously given as conference papers in the *American Journal of Psychology* and in the *Journal of Educational Psychology*, but not in the *Journal of the Experimental Analysis of Behavior*. Brown (2005) found that two-thirds of the papers published in three major accountancy journals had been previously delivered in conferences or workshops. He concluded that:

1   delivering workshop presentations and conference papers increased the probability of getting an initial favourable review ('revise and resubmit' rather than 'reject'); and
2   once such papers were published, they were more influential than were papers that had not been previously presented at conferences.

READING VERSUS SPEAKING

It is important to note that the conference paper is designed to be spoken and listened to; it is not a written paper. There may be a written version for the conference delegates who want one, and for other enquirers, but in the conference itself the focus is on speaking and displaying information. In this connection, Gould (1995, p. 39) remarks that humanists inevitably read their papers from a manuscript, whereas scientists speak extemporaneously from written notes. He also says that scientists nearly always show slides, whereas humanists rely on text alone. These views may be exaggerations, and possibly now out of date, but they are important. Direct speech is clearer than spoken written prose. Thus, it is better to give a conference talk from a set of notes, perhaps prompted by visual aids, than literally to read the paper.

POWERPOINT

Most conference papers these days are accompanied by computer-based slides, and the most common of these use PowerPoint software. Such displays have met with considerable criticism (see Adams, 2006), but it is not all gloom and doom. There is some evidence from students that they like lectures accompanied by PowerPoint presentations (Susskind, 2005) and that slides presented by PowerPoint are preferred to the same materials presented on flip charts and overhead projectors in certain circumstances (e.g. see Austin-Wells et al., 2003). One feature that appeals to an audience is the ability to build up more complex pictures – by adding in more detail on each slide in a series. Students also appreciate the clarity and legibility of PowerPoint presentations, but they dislike poor typographic layouts and odd colour combinations.

Students are not happy either if the lecturer simply reads out the Power-Point slides. One rule of thumb that forces speakers to talk about their slides and not simply to regurgitate them is called the 7 x 7 rule: that is, use no more than seven words per line, and seven lines per slide: (some say 5 x 5). Another way of putting this is to say, 'Write no more on a slide than you would on a postcard'! But suggestions like these bring us back to the criticisms.

The most common criticism of PowerPoint presentations is that the presenters preparing such displays get preoccupied with their format and that, by necessity, they present simplistic arguments. Myers (2000), in an insightful chapter, contrasts giving a conventional lecture (without visual aids) with learning to give the same one with PowerPoint slides. Myers points to a dozen changes overall, leading him to conclude:

> The overall effect is that what was before a carefully connected sequence, with some digressions for stories, and references to texts on a handout, was now a series of spaces, marked by rather flashy transitions.
>
> (Myers, 2000, p. 184)

He continues: 'But these lists of formal changes don't quite get at the shift in effect'. He notes that students now focus on the screen rather than on him, and that:

> I am seen as the animator rather than the source of the utterance. Instead of my speaking with the aid of some visual device, the text is speaking with my aid.
>
> (Myers, 2000, p. 184)

Adams (2006) makes similar criticisms. PowerPoint, it is argued, controls the sequence of presentation (so that it is not easy to respond to an unexpected question), and it makes all the content appear equally significant. PowerPoint it is argued, does not help members of the audience to engage in higher-order thinking and deep understanding. Such arguments, of course, confound the method with the content. Vallance and Towndrow (2007) respond to these criticisms by indicating how one can use PowerPoint alone, and in conjunction with other methods, to achieve more desirable objectives.

THE WRITTEN TEXT

Although the conference paper is delivered orally, it is useful to have a summary version available as a hand-out during the talk. Handouts help listeners follow the presentation and grasp its overall structure. It may be helpful to reproduce copies of any of the key PowerPoint slides, but it is unwise just to present them all in reduced size. The handout needs to be readable, and much is lost if the spoken accompaniment to the slides is omitted. The hand-out should also contain the title of the talk, the speaker's name and institutional address, and the date and place of delivery. These are all useful features for listeners who might want to refer to it at a later date, or to write to the author to ask for an update or further information.

It is also helpful to have a full version of the paper available for distribution at the end of the talk and for later enquirers. Some authors these days do not provide actual copies of their papers at the conferences themselves, but let people know where they can be obtained. As one group of authors put it: 'The first author used to copy and pass out manuscripts at conferences, now she simply passes out a card indicating a www address where interested individuals can access the manuscripts via the Internet' (Murphy *et al.*, 2003, p. 5).

No matter what the format, the conference paper should contain the same features described above for the hand-out. It is indeed remarkable that much of this information is often missing. Table 3.4.1 shows that, in one particular study of conference papers, only half of the papers stated where and when the paper had been delivered, and only half gave a sufficiently detailed contact

Table 3.4.1 Information provided (%) in a sample of 50 conference papers given at the American Educational Research Association's Annual Conference, 2004

	Yes	No
Information on where the paper was delivered	48	52
Contact address in sufficient detail to send for a copy	48	52
Abstract	52	48
References	94	6
Tables and/or figures	78	22
Acknowledgements	6	94

address. Furthermore, when these two features were combined, only twenty-five per cent of the papers had both of these pieces of information.

If you send for a conference paper today, you will find that what you receive may not be an actual copy of what was said at the conference, but rather a more detailed paper upon which the conference presentation was based (Hartley, 2004). What you receive may be a prepublication version of a journal submission or, indeed, a prepublication copy of a future book chapter. This reflects the fact that it is now normal practice for researchers to provide their latest findings on request.

REFERENCES

Adams, C. (2006). PowerPoint, habits of mind, and classroom culture. *Journal of Curriculum Studies*, *38*(4), 398–411.

Austin-Wells, V., Zimmerman, T. & McDougall, G. J. (2003). Determining an optimal delivery format for lectures targeting mature adults. *Educational Gerontology*, *29*(6), 493–501.

Brown, L. D. (2005). The importance of circulating and presenting manuscripts: Evidence from the accounting literature. *The Accounting Review*, *80*(1), 55–83.

Drott, N. C. (1995). Re-examining the role of conference papers. *Journal of the American Society for Information Science*, *46*(4), 299–305.

Gould, S. J. (1995). Ladders and cones: Constraining evolution by canonical icons. In Silvers, R. B. (Ed.), *Hidden histories of science* (pp. 37–67). New York: The New York Review of Books.

Hartley, J. (2004). On requesting conference papers electronically. *Journal of Information Science*, *30*(5), 475–9.

Hartley, J. (2005). Refereeing and the single author. *Journal of Information Science*, *31*(3), 251–6.

Murphy, P. K., Long, J. F., Holleran, T. A. & Esterly, E. (2003). Persuasion online or on paper: A new take on an old issue. *Learning and Instruction*, *13*(5), 511–32.

Myers, G. (2000). Powerpoints: Technology, lectures and changing genres. In A. Trosborg (Ed.), *Analysing professional genres* (pp. 177–91). Amsterdam: John Benjamins.

Schwartz, G. J. & Kennicutt, R. C. (2004). Demographics and citation trends in astrophysical journal papers and pre-prints. 10 November. Retrieved 3 September 2006 from http://arxiv.org/PS-cache/astro-ph/pdf/0411/0411275v1.pdf.

Stolk, P., Egberts, A. C. G. & Leufkens, H. G. M. (2002). Fate of abstracts presented at five international conferences on pharmacoepidemiology (ICPE): 1995–1999. *Pharmacoepidemiology and Drug Safety*, *11*(2), 105–11.

Susskind, J. E. (2005). PowerPoint's power in the classroom: Enhancing students' self-efficacy and attitudes. *Computers & Education*, *45*(2), 203–15.

Vallance, M. & Towndrow, P. A. (2007). Towards the informed use of information and communication technology in education: A response to Adams' 'PowerPoint, habits of mind, and classroom culture.' *Journal of Curriculum Studies*, *39*(2), 219–27.

Weller, A. C. (2002). *Editorial peer review: Its strengths and weaknesses*. Medford, NJ: Information Today.

FURTHER READING

Edirisooriya, G. (1996). Research presentation in a democratic society: A voice from the audience. *Educational Researcher*, *25*(6) 25–30.

Farkas, D. (2006). Toward a better understanding of PowerPoint deck design. *Information Design Journal*, *14*(2), 162–71.

Fischer, B. A. & Zigmond, M. J. (2006). Attending professional meetings successfully. Retrieved 1 September 2006 from www.survival.pitt.edu/library/documents/Attending professionalmeetings-general-2006.pdf.

Hall, G. M. (Ed.) (2007). *How to present at meetings* (2nd edn). BMJ Books, Oxford: Blackwell Publishing.

Kinchin, I. M. (2006). Concept mapping, PowerPoint, and a pedagogy of access. *Journal of Biological Education*, *40*(2), 1–5.

Tables and graphs

Tables and graphs are important features in academic articles and conference papers – and indeed elsewhere. Table 3.5.1 shows the percentage of articles containing tables and graphs in a variety of journals in 2005. Generally speaking there are fewer of these features in journals in the arts and more in journals in the sciences, with the social sciences in between. These data suggest that there is not much to choose between the proportions of authors using *tables* in the sciences and in the social sciences, but that there are differences in how they use *graphs* in this respect. The 'harder', or more scientific the discipline, the greater the use of graphs (Smith *et al.*, 2002).

IMPROVING THE CLARITY OF TABLES

Authors can do a number of things to improve the clarity of tables. These relate to:

1   how they are constructed
2   how they are presented.

Constructing tables

The clarity of tables can be improved by paying attention to their size, complexity and organisation, as well as to the captions and the prose descriptions of the tables that appear in the appropriate parts of the text.

Table 3.5.1 The percentage of articles containing tables and graphs in four different journals in 2005

Journal (2005)	No. of articles	% containing tables	% containing figures	% containing both
J. Educational Psychology	56	96	70	61
American Psychologist	43	47	47	35
Studies in Higher Education	40	55	23	8
J. Scholarly Communication	20	10	0	0

Large tables and figures are comparatively rare in most research articles. Nonetheless, in the 2005 volume of the *Journal of Educational Psychology*, some twenty per cent of the tables occupy whole pages (approximately A4 size). This might be acceptable in an Appendix, but it makes life difficult for readers when such large tables are presented in the body of the text. Furthermore, another ten per cent or so of the tables in this same journal were printed sideways in either the right- or the left-hand column of the two-column page. Readers thus have to reorient the page in order to follow these whilst trying to read the text. As most research articles are available on-screen these days, it is worth thinking more about how to present information in screen-size tables that do not require head/page turning.

The complexity of tables can be reduced by paying attention to some simple rules. Such rules are:

1   split large tables into smaller ones;
2   produce one overall summary table rather than several small tables; for example, Table 2.1.1 (p. 26) summarises the data shown in four tables in the original article;
3   provide clear captions that say what the table is about, or tell the reader what the table shows (some people look at the tables first before reading the text);
4   round off the numbers so that readers can make meaningful comparisons more easily (giving data to four or five decimal points gives a misleading measure of accuracy);
5   consider including averages (averages not only summarise the data but they also allow the reader to grasp better the spread of the scores presented); and
6   use the same layout for a series of tables to avoid subsequent confusion for the reader.

Tables 3.5.2 and 3.5.3 show the effects of rounding. The underlying organisation of a table needs careful thought. The reader needs to be able to grasp this intuitively, or at least quickly, so that data can be retrieved and inferences can be made correctly. Table 3.5.4 shows an original layout that is clarified in Table 3.5.5.

Table 3.5.5 is more successful, because its organisation matches how reading across the table fits in with the language one would use to describe the contents in the text. It is easier to read the productivity scores from left to right in Table 3.5.5, following the labels 'enthusiastic doers' and 'enthusiastic thinkers', than it is following the labels 'thinkers enthusiastic' and 'thinkers anxious' in Table 3.5.4. In addition, higher numbers are placed at the top of Table 3.5.5 rather than at the bottom.

Table 3.5.2 An original table that contravenes rule 2 by giving data too accurately[*]

| | Number of applicants (thousands) | | | |
	1997	2000	2003	2006
Men	159.61	350.73	395.35	399.41
Women	100.31	152.46	220.27	310.64
Total	259.92	503.19	615.62	710.05

* Fictitious data.

Table 3.5.3 The data in Table 3.5.2, rounded up[*]

| | Number of applicants (thousands) | | | |
	1997	2000	2003	2006
Men	160	351	395	399
Women	100	152	220	311
Total	260	503	615	710

* Fictitious data.

Table 3.5.4 The average productivity scores of different kinds of writers[*]

	Enthusiastic	Anxious
Thinkers	20.9	18.1
(N)	(15)	(12)
Doers	32.6	19.8
(N)	(19)	(4)

* Fictitious data.

Table 3.5.5 The data in Table 3.5.4, reorganised to make it easier to read[*]

	Doers	Thinkers
Enthusiastic	32.6	20.9
(N)	(19)	(15)
Anxious	19.8	18.1
(N)	(4)	(12)

* Fictitious data.

Presenting tables

Some ways of printing tables in the text can cause difficulties for readers. One common problem relates to the positioning of the tables on the page. Tables are frequently placed mechanically by typesetters at the top or the bottom of a page (or column), irrespective of where they are mentioned in the text. This can cause difficulties for readers of an article when, say, the last table of the 'results' section appears in the middle of the 'discussion'.

Another related problem is how tables are fitted into the space allocated to them. Tables are typically set to fit the column- or page-width regardless of the effects that this might have upon their clarity. This can cause reading difficulties when a wide table cuts across the middle of a double-column spread. A more serious problem arises when the space between the columns is manipulated to make the table fit the space available, without taking into account whether or not that space is used to group the data appropriately. If, for example, there is more space between the data in the columns headed 'pre-' and 'post-test' for a series of columns, then the reader will group together unrelated data (see Table 3.5.6). Such problems of typesetting can be changed at proof stage – if you ask. There is no need to take them for granted.

Textbooks are available to help authors produce effective tables, ranging from the 'copy this' approach (e.g. Nicol and Pexman, 1999) to more detailed accounts of effective design (e.g. Tufte, 1983).

Prose descriptions of tables

Tables, and their contents, have to be explained to readers in the text. This can partly be done in the caption, but there is usually more to it than this. Salovey (2000) presents contrasting examples (see Table 3.5.7). He argues that the first one is 'statistics-based' and the second one 'reader-based'. In the first passage, we have no idea what was found until the end. In the second one, the findings come first.

Table 3.5.6 The effects of inappropriate internal spacing in a table: readers group together the wrong sets of data[*]

| Condition | School A | | School B | | School C | |
	Pre-test	Post-test	Pre-test	Post-test	Pre-test	Post-test
1	20	25	36	40	51	60
2	21	26	38	42	52	62
3	24	30	42	46	56	63
4	29	32	47	47	59	67
5	28	32	48	58	56	69

* Fictitious data.

Table 3.5.7 Two contrasting descriptions of the contents of a table*

Description 1:
A two-way, 2 x 2 between-subjects ANOVA was performed on ratings of the vividness of childhood memories in which the independent variables were participant sex (male or female) and induced mood (happy or sad). There was no main effect for sex (F (1,99) = 0.20, n.s.), but there was a main effect for mood (F (1,99) = 7.89, p < .01) and a sex by mood interaction (F (1,99) = 12.30, p < .01). Happy people had more vivid memories than sad people, overall. The effect was stronger for women than it was for men. As can be seen in the results from Tukey's studentized range test, reported in Table 1, the vividness of happy and sad female participants' memories differed significantly, but the vividness of happy and sad male participants' memories did not.

Description 2:
Table 1 provides the vividness ratings for men and women who experienced happy or sad moods. The childhood memories of men and women did not differ in vividness, (F (1, 99) = 0.20), n.s. The most striking finding, however, was that the usual tendency for happy people to report more vivid memories than people in sad moods, (F (1, 99) = 7.89, p < .01) was stronger for women than for men, as indicated by a significant sex by mood interaction, (F (1, 99) = 12.30, p < .01). This finding is consistent with the hypothesis that mood has a more pronounced effect upon the quality of childhood memories among women than men and was confirmed with the Tukey's studentized range test reported in Table 1.

---

* From Salovey (2000), pp. 125–6.

Reproduced with permission from the author and Cambridge University Press.

IMPROVING THE CLARITY OF GRAPHS

Problems of typesetting can also affect the appearance of graphs – they too can be squeezed or enlarged to make them fit the space available, and this can affect the perceived importance of the results. And, like tables, graphs too can be separated from where they are first mentioned in the text.

Graphs can also be distorted by their authors – by expanding or contracting the spaces between the measures on the ordinate or the abscissa, or by only focusing on a range of results. Figure 3.5.1 shows the effects of such a strategy.

Pie charts, bar charts and line-graphs

It is usual in discussions such as this to distinguish between pie charts, bar charts and line graphs. Pie charts are much rarer in academic articles than are bar charts and line graphs, and probably should be avoided in this context. Pie charts are difficult to label and to read if they contain several segments (see Figure 3.5.2). Further, multicoloured segments do not copy well in black and white.

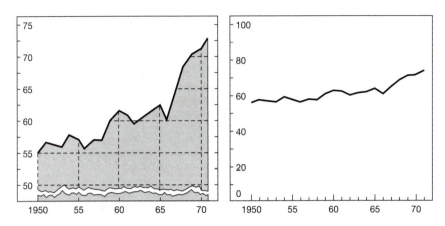

Figure 3.5.1 Plotting the same data with different vertical axes can affect the appearance of a graph and the inferences that are drawn from it (fictitious data).

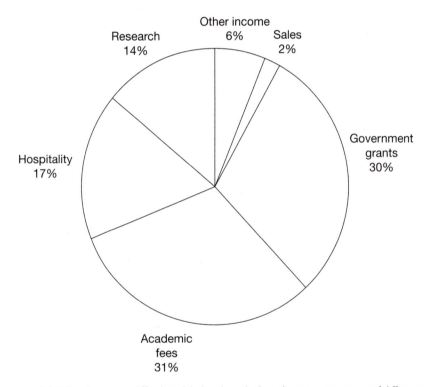

Figure 3.5.2 Pie charts are difficult to label and read when there are segments of different sizes (fictitious data).

Bar charts

Bar charts are easy to construct and are usually clear, but, again, difficulties arise with the labelling if several different components on each measure are presented (in different colours) for separate comparisons. Some authors also seem to forget that what looks clear with separate colours on a computer screen will not look clear in black and white. These difficulties are compounded when authors use computer-based packages to produce three-dimensional (3D) presentations. A sizeable literature now shows that 3D presentations are more confusing than 2D ones (Hartley and Yates, 2001; Mackiewicz, 2007). Figure 3.5.3 shows the differences that ensue, even on a simple chart.

Line graphs

Line graphs are good for showing, say, the performance of two or more groups in different conditions, especially when the data from the different groups vary according to the condition they are in – technically, when there is an 'interaction' between them. Figure 3.5.4 shows such an interaction that it is hard to describe in words and that is also sometimes difficult to detect in a table of numbers. However, line graphs can provide difficulties for readers when there are multiple groups (say, more than three) in multiple conditions (say, more than three).

Tables and graphs thus provide different ways of presenting data, each with their advantages and disadvantages. Writers need to think carefully about which method will be easiest for their readers to understand. Tables are probably best for displaying exact numbers; graphs for displaying trends in the data. As with tables, there are a number of useful texts on graphing techniques (e.g. see Nicol and Pexman, 2003; Tufte, 1983). A key concept introduced by Tufte (1983) is that writers should avoid the use of 'chart-junk' – all those embellishments that add clutter to a display.

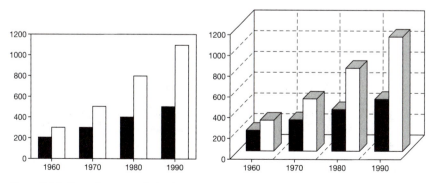

Figure 3.5.3 Two-dimensional displays are easier to read than are three-dimensional displays of the same data (fictitious data).

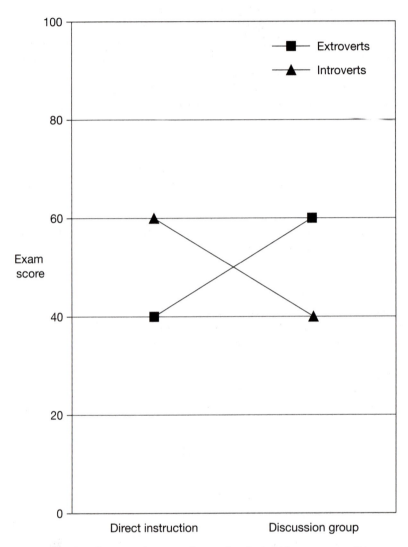

Figure 3.5.4 An interaction between the results obtained from two conditions
           (methods of instruction) and two groups (introverts and extroverts).*

* Fictitious data.

TABLES AND GRAPHS IN CONFERENCE PRESENTATIONS

Many of the features of tables and graphs discussed above are also relevant to their presentation in conferences. However, in conference presentations, it is best to present data drastically simplified – complexities can be covered in the talk. For conference presentations, tables and figures need to be an adequate size and to use few, possibly only two, contrasting colours (e.g. dark text on a pale background, or the reverse of this for darkened rooms). Full explanatory captions or titles on each slide also help (Alley *et al.*, 2006).

REFERENCES

Alley, M., Schreiber, M., Ramsdell, K. & Muffo, J. (2006). How the design of headlines in presentation slides affects audience retention. *Technical Communication*, 53(2), 1–10.

Hartley, J. & Yates, P. (2001). Referees are not always right! The case of the 3-D graph. *British Journal of Educational Technology*, 32(5), 623–6.

Mackiewicz, J. (2007). Perceptions of clarity and attractiveness in PowerPoint graph slides. *Technical Communication*, 54(2), 145–56.

Nicol, A. A. M. & Pexman, P. M. (1999). *Presenting your findings: A practical guide for creating tables*. Washington, DC: American Psychological Association.

Nicol, A. A. M. & Pexman, P. M. (2003). *Displaying your findings: A practical guide for creating figures, posters and presentations*. Washington, DC: American Psychological Association.

Salovey, P. (2000). Results that get results: Telling a good story. In R. J. Sternberg (Ed.), *Guide to publishing in psychology journals* (pp. 121–32). Cambridge: Cambridge University Press.

Smith, L. D., Best, L. A., Stubbs, D. A., Archibald, A. B. & Robertson-Nay, A. (2002). Constructing knowledge: The role of graphs and tables in hard and soft psychology. *American Psychologist*, 57(10), 749–61.

Tufte, E. R. (1983). *The visual display of quantitative data*. Cheshire, CT 06410: Graphics Press.

FURTHER READING

Few, S. (2006). *Information dashboard design: The effective visual communication of data*. Sebastopol, CA: O'Reilly.

Hartley, J. (2007). Guiding the copy editor: Positioning tables and figures in the text. *PsyPag Quarterly Newsletter*, Issue 63, June, pp. 54–9.

Posters

Poster papers were initially introduced to ensure that people could still have their work presented at conferences when there was insufficient space for it on the main programme. Curiously enough, I have been unable to find any assessments of their effectiveness in this respect.

Most papers on posters concern their design. Figure 3.6.1 shows a typical arrangement for a poster at a scientific conference. Conference organisers usually specify how large such posters can be. A conventional size is about 4 feet (120 cm) wide by 2.5 feet (75 cm) deep, but this can vary. It is essential, therefore, to find out what size is allowed before designing a poster.

Some suggestions for presentation, culled from various papers are:

- Have a clear, short title.
- Avoid acronyms in the title (and the text).
- Use a large type size (24–30 point). (Try reading your poster – or someone else's – from 3 to 6 feet away.)
- Use no more than three columns of text and make the flow/organisation of the text clear. Some readers will expect to go across the columns and some down. Using the IMRAD structure for the sub-headings, if appropriate, is helpful in this regard.
- Do not use all capital letters for headings, titles, etc.
- Do not underline headings.
- Use only one or two type-faces.
- Set the text 'unjustified', that is, from the left in each column, with equal word spacing and a ragged right-hand edge (as here).
- Use short sentences and 'bulleted' lists.
- Do not set the text single-spaced.
- Use one, two or at most only three colours, and only if each colour has a didactic purpose.
- Do not use 3D graphics (see p. 107).
- Supplement your poster with a summary handout and/or a full paper that includes your name and address and the date and place of the presentation. This can be given to enquirers and people who pass by.

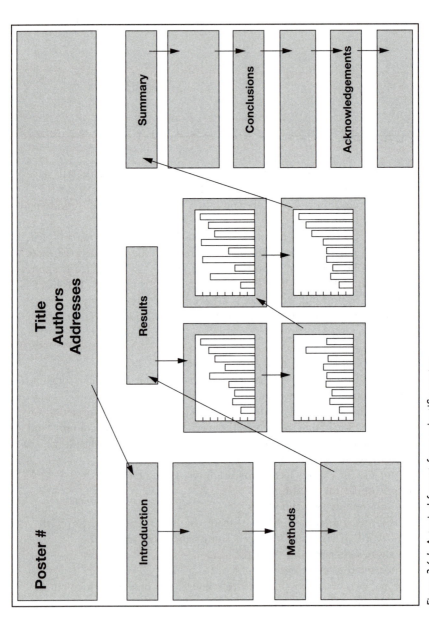

Figure 3.6.1 A typical format for a scientific poster.

Reproduced with permission of Betch Fischer and Zigmond (2006), available at www.survival.pitt.edu.

Most poster presenters offend at least one or more of these rules. In particular, people seem reluctant to cut their material down to make it accessible on a poster, or to remember that text is hard to read from a distance. Even award-winning posters can be improved in this respect.

REFERENCE

Fischer, B. A. & Zigmond, M. J. (2006). Attending professional meetings successfully. Retrieved 11 July 2007 from www.survival.pitt.edu.

FURTHER READING

Nicol, A. A. M. & Pexman, P. M. (2003). *Displaying your findings: A practical guide for creating figures, posters and presentations*. Washington, DC: American Psychological Association.

Matthews, D. L. (1990). The scientific poster: Guidelines for effective visual communication. *Technical Communication*, 37(3rd Quarter), 225–32.

Book reviews

Book reviews play an important part in academic communication. Most academic journals publish book reviews in addition to their articles and, indeed, some journals publish nothing but book reviews.

Book reviews are a special form of academic writing. They have well-known structures with familiar components. When writing book reviews, colleagues use a variety of phrases that carry hidden meanings (see Table 3.7.1).

Book reviews differ from academic articles submitted for publication because, in the main, they are solicited by an editor and are not subject to the normal refereeing process. Editors normally accept for publication the reviews that are submitted (although they may sometimes shorten them).

CHOOSING THE REVIEWERS

Different editors have different procedures for choosing book reviewers. Some, for example, maintain panels of authors deemed appropriate for the task, whereas others work more with their personal knowledge of authors in their field, perhaps guided by recommendations from colleagues.

Today, there are several journals where the editors do not personally select individual authors to review a particular book. Here, lists of books received for review are distributed by email attachments to a panel of reviewers and/or readers, who can then select any that interest them (e.g. *PsycCRITIQUES*, *British Journal of Educational Technology*). Completed book reviews are submitted by email or downloaded directly using electronic editing software. One or two journals provide electronic templates for their reviewers to follow when writing their reviews (e.g. *International Journal of Commerce and Management*).

WRITING BOOK REVIEWS: EDITORIAL INSTRUCTIONS

Because book reviews are not normally refereed, editors need to make clear what they require. Thus, there are usually instructions on these matters for

Table 3.7.1 The hidden meanings of phrases in book reviews

'This is a surprising book'
> *This is better than expected*

'A mixed bag'
> *Not much in this but one or two chapters worth thinking about*

'A useful book for the library'
> *Not very exciting*

'The discussion is somewhat abstruse'
> *I could not understand much of this*

'For the most part this is a thorough, lucid and well-argued book but a few weaknesses can be noted. First . . .'
> *That's done the praise bit, now let's get down to the criticisms*

'In my view more scholarly references would be better for the readers of this text than the par-boiled information referred to on web sites'
> *This is a light weight text* and/or
> *My scholarship is superior to that of the authors*

'The author has presented opposing views fairly, although instances of bias are detectable by the omission of some critical references'
> *He has left out my key paper on . . .*

'This is a useful account of unastonishing work'
> *Oh dear . . .*

(Last sentence) 'The authors' position leads them to omit key research and to propose work that is complex and interesting but which will not improve the education of children'
> *Ouch!*

Bressler (1999) comments: 'The reviewer is able to compress complex ideas into a snappy 600 words and to substitute veiled allusion for systematic argument because he can trust his readers to decipher the message'. (p. 709)

Updated from Hartley (2006). Reprinted with permission of John Wiley & Sons, Inc. © James Hartley, 2006.

potential book reviewers. Such instructions typically cover technical matters, and content.

Guidance on technical matters

These instructions often start with an indication of the required length: 'Individual book reviews should be between 800 and 1,200 words in length, depending upon the amount of attention which you feel the book merits'. Indeed, advice about length is sometimes the only advice given.

There may, however, be further advice on layout: 'Reviews should be set justified and double-spaced'. In some journals a good deal of attention is given to how to head the review in the appropriate format for that particular journal (e.g. author – surname first – date of publication, title – in bold, place of publication, publisher, number of pages, ISBN number, price). Similarly, there are sometimes instructions on how to end the review, with the reviewer's name and institutional affiliation, and perhaps a request for some biographical notes.

Much space is devoted in some editorial instructions on to how cite quotations from the book being reviewed, and on how to provide references and/or footnotes. However, some journals explicitly forbid such details: 'Please use references only sparingly, if at all' (*The Psychologist*). Finally, there are instructions for submitting the finished review: for example 'Please send your review by 6th August to meet the November deadline.'

Guidance on content

Some journals provide more advice. The *Journal of the Medical Library Association*, for example, provides potential book reviewers with lengthy notes on the aims and scope of the journal, together with a paragraph on what the content of the review might contain:

> Reviews should contain a brief overview of the scope and content [of the book being reviewed] so that readers can determine the book's interest to them. Reviewing each chapter of a book is not necessary. For a research or historical work, please comment on its significance in relation to the focus area as well as to the field as a whole. For an applied or descriptive work, be sure to comment on its usefulness. In both cases compare the book with similar publications in its area and indicate its potential audiences, where relevant.

Other journals go further, for example:

> The editor encourages reviewers to devote special attention to the political assumptions and discussions in the book under review.
>
> (*Law and Politics Book Review*)

There are also – sometimes – suggestions about style:

> We are seeking reviews that are incisive . . . integrative . . . balanced . . . and provocative.
>
> (*PsycCRITIQUES*)

> It is not required that every review contain at least one negative remark. Selective detail is refreshing. Encyclopaedic detail – as in a chapter by chapter outline – is rarely called for.
>
> (*American Journal of Physics*)

One or two journals remark on the possibility that a reviewer, having examined a book, may not wish to review it. Such books should be returned for re-assignment. Others comment on ethical matters:

> Professional ethics require that you do not review a book when an overriding sense of personal obligation, competition or enmity exists.
> (*Law and Politics Book Review*)

Nature requires its book reviewers to sign certain disclaimers (e.g. that they have not been in dispute with the book's author) before their review can be published.

Unsolicited book reviews

Some editors accept unsolicited reviews, provided that they meet the required standards. As one editor put it:

> I strongly encourage unsolicited reviews.
> (*Journal of Technical Writing and Communication*)

Others are more cautious, for example:

> This journal does not publish unsolicited reviews. However, if you would like to be added to our database of potential reviewers, please fill in our potential reviewers data-sheet.
> (*The Hispanic American Historical Review*)

Some editors are more blunt:

> Unsolicited book reviews are not accepted.
> (*American Historical Review*)

READING AND WRITING BOOK REVIEWS

In a recent study, I reported on my findings when I sent out an electronic questionnaire on reading and writing book reviews to groups of academics in the arts, sciences and social sciences (Hartley, 2006).

Approximately fifty people in each of these groups replied. Almost two-thirds of them recalled reading a dreadful book review. Some of the things they said about such reviews were that they were:

- pointless, uninformative, indecisive and boring
- a mere listing of the contents

- pretentious, unkind and careless
- personally abusive about the author's credentials
- written to cherish the reviewer's ego.

Generally speaking, book reviews were not highly regarded if they simply outlined the content of a book using a chapter by chapter format.

On the other hand, approximately half of the respondents recalled reading an outstanding book review. Here they thought that such reviews:

- gave a balanced, critical evaluation of the text
- made seemingly dull topics interesting
- were well written, succinct and informative
- made theoretical contributions in their own right
- made people want to buy the book.

In a wide-ranging and informative paper, Miranda (1996) suggests that the key features of successful reviews are that the reviewer:

- evaluates the contribution of the text
- sets the work in a larger, broader context
- identifies the strengths and weaknesses of the arguments
- involves the reader in the discussion.

Miranda also notes that some book review formats are not used as extensively as they might be. She distinguishes between *integrated formats*, where there are several reviews on books on the same subject matter; *multidisciplinary format*, where one book is reviewed by people from different disciplines; *special issue formats*, where the reviews supplement and complement the theme of selected papers in that issue of the journal; *review essay sections*, where two or three books on the same or contrasting themes are reviewed by the same reviewer; and *rejoinders*, where a review is followed by the author's reply. All of these formats seem worth exploring more.

How then do authors write book reviews? Respondents to my questionnaire were reluctant to commit themselves. Most argued that it depended on the book in question. One, however, wrote: 'I use a basic sort of "recipe" that touches on all the information that I think readers of book reviews need'.

Two stages appear to be required. First of all, there is the preliminary reading and thinking about the book. Sometimes this is done before starting on the review, but some reviewers start making notes from the outset. At this stage, reviewers are concerned with selecting and thinking about information that will be relevant to the task. This might involve a trip to the library or to particular web sites to check up on required information.

Next comes the actual writing of the review. Here, different writers have different preferences. The quotations given in Figure 3.7.1 provide but two examples.

'I usually read completely the books I am reviewing (so as to be sure that I do not misunderstand them), marking parts that I think are particularly meaningful. Then I start by saying what the book is about and the intended audience (since having this information first may allow readers who are not interested to skip the rest of the review, and readers who are interested to raise their attention). Next I outline how the topic is developed, as concerns facets of content and depth of treatment. Then I point out what are in my opinion the points of strengths and weaknesses of the book. Finally, I try to give a global evaluation of my appreciation and possible usefulness of the book. Finally I polish the form and try to bring it to the required length. This writing phase lasts usually around two hours'.

'I read the book through, marking on it possible points for inclusion on (i) what the author says the book is about, (ii) possible key findings, and (iii) controversial statements. I then decide on which of these to include and which bits of the book to write about and what to leave out (because of space limitations). I word-process the first draft, which is usually too long, and then I cut it and continually refine it through numerous editings – with periods for incubation between each one – until it emerges, in my view, as a highly polished piece of prose!'

Figure 3.7.1 Examples of how academics write book reviews.

From Hartley (2006), p. 1203. Reprinted with permission of John Wiley & Sons, Inc. © James Hartley, 2006.

Whatever the procedure, it is important that a book review contains a number of key features. Figure 3.7.2 provides a checklist that might prove useful in this respect.

Make sure that your review contains:

- ☐ An early paragraph saying what the book is about, and putting it in context
- ☐ Information about the intended audience
- ☐ A critique of the argument/content of the book
- ☐ Any supporting academic references
- ☐ Remarks on the strengths and limitations of the book
- ☐ A note on the format, length and price (or value for money)
- ☐ A note (if appropriate) on how well the text is supported by tables/diagrams/illustrations

If the following details are not supplied for you, please make sure that your review contains:

- ☐ Accurate details of the authors'/editors' names and initials
- ☐ Title of the publication
- ☐ Edition
- ☐ Date of publication
- ☐ Publisher and place of publication
- ☐ ISBN number
- ☐ Format (hardback, paperback or soft cover)
- ☐ Number of pages
- ☐ Price

Figure 3.7.2 A checklist for book reviewers.

From Hartley (2006), p. 1205. Reprinted with permission of John Wiley & Sons, Inc. © James Hartley, 2006.

REFERENCES

Bressler, M. (1999). Contemporary Sociology: A quarter century of book reviews. *Sociological Forum*, *14*(4), 707–20.

Hartley, J. (2006). Reading and writing book reviews across the disciplines. *Journal of the American Society for Information Science and Technology*, *57*(9), 1194–207.

Miranda, E. O. (1996). On book reviewing. *Journal of Educational Thought*, *30*(2), 191–202.

FURTHER READING

Lindholm-Romantschuk, Y. (1998). *Scholarly book reviewing in the Social Sciences and Humanities: The flow of ideas within and amongst disciplines*. Westport, CT: Greenwood Press.

Hyland, K. (2004). *Disciplinary discourses: Social interactions in academic writing.* Ann Arbor, MI: University of Michigan Press.

Nicolaisen, J. (2002). The scholarliness of published peer reviews: A bibliometric study of book reviews in selected social science fields. *Research Evaluation, 11*(3), 129–40.

Chapter 3.8

Letters to the editor

Sometimes it strikes you, when reading a recently published paper, that the authors have failed to include some important variable, made a statistical error or omitted a key research finding. One way of responding to this is to write a letter to the editor, or a short note for publication.

Letters to the editor typically follow the following format or 'moves' (Magnet and Carnet, 2006). They:

- start with 'Sir/Madam'
- remind the reader of the contents of the paper to be commented on
- raise the explicit criticism
- give evidence for the criticism
- urge colleagues not to take at face value the specific point made in the earlier paper.

Although not real letters in the accepted sense, letters to the editor are typically written in the first person. They are more likely to use disparaging terms to belittle the point made in the paper to which they are responding (e.g. *poorly conceived, mistaken, not well thought out, inappropriate, unsupported,* etc.) and 'boosters' to strengthen their own position (e.g. *show clearly, demonstrate, confirm the fact that,* etc.) (Hyland, 2004).

According to Magnet and Carnet (2006), letters to the editor are not refereed, have a higher acceptance rate, and are usually published more quickly than are original articles, but this is in medicine. In my own experience, I have found that most, if not all, of the letters that I have written have been politely received, even welcomed, but not published for one reason or another (e.g. 'insufficient space', 'the matter is in hand', etc.).

Figure 3.8.1 provides an example of one of my letters to an editor. Needless to say it was not published.

Magnet and Carnet maintain that, although such letters may seem to serve as a device for writers to let off steam, they play an important part in scientific communication. They argue that such letters can suggest ways of redirecting research, indicate new paths to explore and foster future

Dear Sir,

Confusion in the sub-headings of structured abstracts

Structured abstracts for articles in medical journals typically use five sub-headings: 'Background', 'Aim', 'Method', 'Results' and 'Conclusions' (1). The authors of articles written for XXXX, however, are not required to specify the 'Aim' of their studies, but simply to give the 'Background' (2). However, I maintain that the five sub-headings are better than the four you recommend because the single heading 'Background' does not help authors to distinguish between the background to a study ('Previous research has suggested . . .') and the question under current investigation ('The aim of this study was to . . .').

I demonstrated this elsewhere when I examined the contents under the sub-heading 'Background' for 100 articles in the British Journal of Psychiatry (3). Here 37% of the articles gave the background alone, 26% gave the aims alone, and 37% gave both the background and the aims.

It is too early yet to examine many abstracts written under the 2006 rubric for XXXX. But if one examines on the XXXX Website the abstracts for the articles published in June 2006, 17 used five or more sub-headings, 15 used four, 1 used three, and 7 were unstructured. For the 15 abstracts with four sub-headings, 6 used the heading 'Study Objective(s), 4 'Objective(s)', 3 'Background', 1 'Background and Study Objectives' and 1, 'Introduction'.

The data show that there is confusion over the wording and the contents of structured abstracts in XXXX. Greater clarity can be achieved by requiring five sub-headings so that authors have to indicate separately both the background and the aim of their papers.

1 Hartley J. Clarifying the abstracts of systematic literature reviews. Bull.Med.Libr. Assoc. 2 000; 84: 332–336.
2 Instruction to authors. Downloaded from XXXX website on 14 June 2006.
3 Hartley J. Headings in structured abstracts. Brit.J.Psychiat. 1998; 173: 178.

Figure 3.8.1 An example of a letter to an editor.

collaborations. Not everyone would agree, however. Horton (2002), for instance, traced the effects of critical letters to the *Lancet* on three topics. Each of these had attracted twelve or more critical letters to the editor. Horton noted that, in the original authors' replies, more than half of the criticisms went unanswered, and that important weaknesses detected in the letters were ignored in subsequently published practice guidelines . . .

SHORT NOTES

Another genre for responding to previous research is the 'short note'. Such notes may be less disparaging than the letter to the editor and possibly a lot longer. The same stages outlined above for letters may again be present in the note, but normally with more detail. Such notes are likely to be refereed, and often there are replies from the original authors. Short notes can also be used to make a particular point in general, rather than target a specific person. Short notes are accepted as 'rapid responses' to articles on some journal web sites, and new readers can be directed to them when they download the original article (e.g. see *http://bmj.com*).

REFERENCES

Horton, R. (2002). Postpublication criticism and the shaping of clinical knowledge. *Journal of the American Medical Association, 287*(21), 2843–7.

Hyland, K. (2004). *Disciplinary discourses: Social interactions in academic writing.* Ann Arbor, MI: University of Michigan Press.

Magnet, A. & Carnet, D. (2006). Letters to the editor: Still vigorous after all these years? A presentation of the discursive and linguistic features of the genre. *English for Specific Purposes, 25*(2), 173–99.

FURTHER READING

Leong, S. C. L. (2006). Letters to the editor: Publish or perish. *Clinical Otolaryngology, 31*(4), 350–2.

Annotated bibliographies

It is a curious thing that we learn more from other people's mistakes than from their successes. I had not thought to include a chapter in this book on annotated bibliographies but was drawn to do so by coming across a bad example.

This bibliography was unhelpful because it did not group the titles in clusters of meaningful topics, and it did not offer any commentary on most of the individual entries. Good annotated bibliographies group entries in some way or another – for example, by method (experimental studies . . ., qualitative studies . . ., short reports . . .) or by age (studies with children . . ., studies with adolescents . . ., studies with parents . . .). This particular example did not do this. After a brief introduction, mentioning some thirty works, a list of over 200 titles was presented in alphabetical order determined by first author's surname. Furthermore, where no author was quoted (putting 'anon' would be appropriate), the first word of the *title* determined the position of the entry in the list. Thus 'Guide to . . .', 'How to . . .', 'In this issue . . .', etc., became separate alphabetically related entries. In short, the list had no perceivable structure.

Further, the entries seemed to have been culled from contents' pages of some of the appropriate journals for the topic, but not from all of them. Indeed, entries from the journal in which the bibliography appeared were singularly missing, but there were no entries from other well-known journals in the list that claimed to be a list of publications in the field from 2001 to 2005. Good annotated bibliographies are more selective in their choice of entries and cover the full range of relevant publications.

Indeed, it is the commentary in an annotated bibliography that is the important thing. Anyone can find titles by using an appropriate search engine, but judgements about the quality of the contents are harder to come by.

Many writers (and Ph.D. students) maintain a list of publications in their field (see Chapter 4.1). Publishing a brief list of the key books, chapters and papers in a particular field, each with a brief commentary, can be extremely helpful for other authors and students anxious to find out what is available.

Other aspects of academic writing

Finding, keeping and disseminating information

The World Wide Web has revolutionised how academics find information. In writing this book I have not had to venture far from my office. The information that I have used to write each chapter has mainly come from books on my shelves, papers stored in my filing cabinets, previous papers on the topic that I have written, and papers located in databases and electronic journals on the Web. In searching these latter resources, I have roamed well beyond my own discipline. Only occasionally have I had to resort to the library and the inter-library loan service – mainly for books.

Junni (2007) remarks that the Internet is an attractive medium for seeking and obtaining information for the following reasons:

- It is accessible twenty-four hours a day.
- You do not have to visit a library.
- It is possible to find and obtain information relatively quickly and conveniently.
- You can choose between saving, printing or reading the information from the computer screen.
- Sources on the Internet are often more up to date than sources in paper format.

Bjork and Turk (2002) report on how, for scientists, the Internet is overtaking paper media, and that the most popular method for retrieving a publication is to download it for free from authors' or publishers' web sites. The ways that scientists retrieve information differ, of course, from those used by researchers in the arts and humanities, and in the social sciences. Jankowska (2004) showed, as expected, that scientists used the Internet more frequently than did social scientists, and that social scientists used it more frequently than did members of the arts. Vakkari and Talja (2006) found that Finnish academics used key-word searching more frequently in the natural sciences, engineering and medicine than in other disciplines, and that they all relied less on colleagues for finding information than they used to.

There has been some debate about the relative usefulness of different search engines for different tasks. Bar-Ilan (2005), for instance, compared Google, Yahoo and MSN on a huge variety of tasks, and found considerable differences between them. However, one difficulty with this kind of research is that web sites are constantly being updated, and newer ones introduced. (Google Scholar or Microsoft's Windows Live Academic Research, for instance, were not available to Bar-Ilan when this research was done.) Other studies have looked at the effectiveness of individual search engines for providing the different kinds of information needed by researchers. Valiela and Martinetto (2005), for instance, found that it was difficult to locate papers published before the 1970s by well-known authors on the ecology of aquatic environments, but that the position was much better for more recent publications. However, they too found that there was considerable variability between the success rates achieved for both early and later papers on different web sites. Furthermore, the value of all the 'hits' listed on a web site in response to a specific query needs to be taken with a pinch of salt (Jacso, 2006).

A more promising development in this area perhaps lies in the creation of electronic databases for specific disciplines. Mann *et al.* (2006), for instance, describe one such database that contains over 300,000 publications in computer science, and the Social Science Information Gateway (SOSIG) publishes booklets that list key databases in a variety of subjects (www. sosig.ac.uk). Using such databases, it is possible to find the most important papers, the earliest and the latest papers, and work in your own and related fields.

Finally, other sources of information that researchers need to keep an eye on are preprints. Schwartz and Kennicutt (2004) reported that seventy-two per cent of the papers in *Astro-Physics Journal* (*Ap-J*) were posted as *astro-ph* preprints, and that papers posted on *astro-ph* were cited twice as often as papers that were not posted. They concluded that, 'Pre-prints have clearly supplanted the journals as the primary means for initially becoming aware of papers, at least for a large fraction of the *Ap-J* author community'. Indeed, it is now becoming common practice for journals to publish online copies of articles that are to appear in print somewhat later. Email 'alert' systems allow researchers to obtain and download these papers in advance, and reading such alerts is much akin to browsing in the library in olden times.

Indeed, one can browse on the Internet too. I have found it particularly useful, for instance, to locate papers on Google Scholar, to trace them back to the journal where they first appeared and to see who has cited them and/or written articles on similar topics. Chasing up authors' email addresses and web pages too can lead to lists of further publications that might be relevant to the task at hand or just of general interest.

KEEPING INFORMATION

One of the many problems of being an academic is keeping track of information that might be useful in the future. Basically, this means setting up an effective storage and retrieval system. Initially, this may not seem important. Young researchers are likely to be working in a single field, and they will have most of the relevant papers at their finger-tips, but, as you get older, it gets more complex, both starting new areas of research and keeping up with old ones.

So what is needed is some way of storing relevant publications. In my research, I use a now old-fashioned system. I code with a number a copy of any paper that I wish to store, and I file it sequentially. I then enter the appropriate number in a card subject index. So, if I want to see if I have any papers on, say, 'titles', I look up 'titles' in the subject index, find the numbers and retrieve the relevant papers from the file. Using this card system allows me to expand the subject index appropriately as new but relevant materials appear. Using the unique number system allows me to enter the same number on different cards if the paper touches on different topics.

Well, that is how it started. I then found that I began to place copies of related papers in separate folders and, in turn, as these folders grew too small, into separate boxes. So now I have a card filing system with more than 2,500 entries, about fifty folders and twenty or so boxes . . .

It would be more useful these days to have a less bulky electronic system. It would be nice to look up topics (with a key-word system) and to print out the relevant papers when required. Google Scholar provides an example, but it does not have the selectivity or permanence of my paper system, and it is a bit hit and miss. And, as noted above, different search engines have different strengths in this respect.

New technology presents an additional problem. It is now easier to locate materials using the World Wide Web and specific search engines, but there is far more of it. This means that the materials required for storage are going to be more bulky if they are printed out (although this can be reduced by printing only the abstracts and keeping the URL).

I asked a number of postgraduates at Keele about how they keep track of relevant information today. The following extracts from three replies indicate that this ranges from doing nothing systematic to saving journals as PDF files.

- *Student 1*: My method of storing information is so disorganised that you definitely would not want to include it as an example. (Unless it is an example of how **not** to do it!)
- *Student 2*: When I first started at university, I obtained lots of articles, but did not use any specific filing method to keep them in order. A fellow Ph.D. student urged me to start putting my references into

Reference Manager, so I could keep track, but I'm afraid I didn't take his advice and acquired a large number of articles that were becoming increasingly unordered on my desk! Eventually, I thought I should come up with some kind of system otherwise I wasn't going to be able to keep track. When I actually started using the program to manage my references, I felt stupid for not having done it before.

- *Student 3*: From the start of my Ph.D. I used Reference Manager. I decided to use this method because we had a training course on it and I realised that I needed a formal way of storing my references. I also thought I would need to use such a system right from the start so that I would get into a routine . . . When it came to writing up papers and my thesis it was much easier to do having put all my references in Reference Manager.

   Now that many of the journals are available online I also save some of the journals on my computer as PDF files. I find that it makes journals really accessible. I also like the fact that I don't have to physically print them off if I don't want to, but I can still access them. This method has the advantages of saving space and is thus more environmentally friendly.

Although there were some studies of how academics organised their papers in the past, there is relatively little work of this kind with new technology. The paper by Khoo *et al.* (2007) is therefore of interest. Khoo *et al.* interviewed twelve professionals about how they managed and organised their electronic files on their computer hard disk at their workplace and scanned the disk in question. The majority of these people stored files both on their desktops as well as in folders on their hard drive. The desktop tended to be used for ephemeral or temporary files, as well as for working files in current projects. Some of the participants positioned their files on the desktop spatially, and some chronologically. All of the participants organised their folders and sub-folders in a variety of tree-like structures, with a considerable range in the number and the depth. Most of the participants were 'frequent filers', who stored documents in appropriate folders immediately, or 'spring cleaners', who cleaned up and tidied file documents into folders more periodically.

Finding and keeping track of relevant information is perhaps easier than it was in my day, but knowing how to cope with what you find is more daunting. One solution, perhaps, might be not to store anything, but simply look up the latest findings on the Web when starting something new and when writing it up. However, this, I think, is both unscholarly and premature. A chance reading of a paper on the topic of the effects of headings in text prompted me to look up how many papers I had on this topic in my files, how many were cited on Google Scholar, and how many of these were available in both sources. I found twenty studies cited in the first ten pages of Google

Scholar, forty-two in my files, and an overlap of only six papers between them. Each of these separate papers, of course, had its own additional reference list . . .

USING THE INFORMATION

There have been few studies of how authors integrate materials from the Internet with that published in scientific articles. Junni (2007) examined the reference lists in masters' theses in economics, psychology and mathematics, written in Finland in 1985, 1993 and 2003, and carried out semi-structured interviews with a selection of students who had completed their theses in 2003. Junni found that the average number of *items* in the reference lists in the economics and psychology theses had increased between 1993 and 2003; that the average number of *scholarly articles* referenced in the economics and psychology theses had increased between 1993 and 2003; and that the average number of *recent* articles cited had increased in the psychology and mathematics theses. Junni attributed these differences to the fact that the availability of articles had increased dramatically for students and researchers via the Internet, and that the sources on the Internet were generally more up to date than were those in paper format.

DISSEMINATING INFORMATION

In the good old days, authors typically sent preprints, or early drafts of their articles, to friends and colleagues and to interested enquirers. Today, most authors supply lists of their publications on the Web or, indeed, make the publications themselves available on the Web. This is extremely helpful for researchers, provided that the lists are regularly updated.

One point of interest here is that if you provide a web-based URL it might also be useful to include what is called the digital object identifier (DOI) number. The DOI number for online publications is similar to the ISBN number for books and the ISSN number for journals: it is a unique number for the document. URLs do not identify the document itself but only its location – and, as we all know to our chagrin, this may change, and the document may become irretrievable.

REFERENCES

Bar-Ilan, J. (2005). Expectations versus reality – Search engine features needed for Web research at mid 2005. Retrieved 18 October 2006 from *Cybermetrics*, *9*(1), paper 2 (page numbers unspecified) (www.cindoc.csic.es/cybermetrics/)

Bjork, B-C. & Turk, Z. (2002). How scientists retrieve publications: An empirical study of how the Internet is overtaking paper media. Retrieved 20 October 2006 from the *Journal of Electronic Publishing*, *6*(2) (page numbers unspecified) (www.press.umich.edu/jep/06-02/bjork.html).

Jacso, P. (2006). Google Scholar and *The Scientist*. Retrieved 6 January 2006 from www2.hawaii.edu/~jacso/extra/gs/.

Jankowska, M. A. (2004). Identifying university professors' information needs in the challenging environment of information and communication technologies. *Journal of Academic Librarianship*, *30*(1), 51–66.

Junni, P. (2007). Students seeking information for their Masters' theses: The effect of the Internet. Retrieved 18 July 2007 from *Information Research*, *12*(2), paper 305 (http://InformationR.net/ir/12-2paper305.html).

Khoo, C., Luyt, B., Ee, C., Osman, J., Lim, H. H. & Yound, S. (2007). How users organize electronic files on their workstations in the office environment: A preliminary study of personal information organization behaviour. Retrieved 18 July 2007 from *Information Research*, *12*(2), paper 293 (page numbers unspecified) (http://InformationR.net/ir/12-2paper293.html).

Mann, G., Mimno, D. & McCallum, A. (2006). Bibliometric impact measures leveraging topic analysis. *Proceedings of the 6th ACM / IEEE-CS Joint Conference on Digital Libraries* (pp. 65–74). Chapel Hill, NJ: ACM Press.

Schwartz, G. J. & Kennicutt, R. C. (2004). Demographics and citation trends in astrophysical journal papers and pre-prints. 10 November. Retrieved 3 September 2006 from http://arxiv.org/PS-cache/astro-ph/pdf/0411/0411275v1.pdf.

Vakkari, P. & Talja, S. (2006). Searching for electronic journal articles to support academic tasks. A case study of the use of the Finnish National Electronic Library (finELib). Retrieved 20 July 2007 from *Information Research*, *12*(1), paper 285 (page numbers unspecified) (http://InformationR.net/ir/12-1/paper285.html).

Valiela, I. & Martinetto, P. (2005). The relative ineffectiveness of bibliographic search engines. *Bioscience*, *55*(8), 688–92.

FURTHER READING

Case, D. O. (2002). *Looking for information: A survey of research on information seeking, needs, and behavior*. San Diego, CA: Academic Press.

Xu, Y., Tan, C. Y & Yang, L. (2006). Who will you ask? An empirical study of interpersonal task information seeking. *Journal of the American Society for Information Science & Technology*, *57*(12), 1666–77.

Choosing where to publish

At the time of writing (June 2007), it is estimated that there are around 20,000–25,000 peer-reviewed academic journals published worldwide, and that approximately ninety per cent of journals in the UK and the USA are published online (although most of these have parallel print versions). So – in some subjects – there are many journals to choose between when publishing an article. Key factors affecting choice appear to be impact factors, reputation and relevance.

IMPACT AND OTHER FACTORS

Researchers are encouraged these days to submit their articles to journals with high 'impact factors'. Such journals, it is claimed, are of better quality than those with low impact factors, and this will stand them in better stead in any evaluation of their research (however this is done).

The impact factor of a journal is found by dividing the number of *citations* in one year to articles in the previous two years in that particular journal by the number of *articles* published by that journal in the two preceding years. Thus, if in 2007 there were 130 citations to articles in the *American Psychologist* in 2006 and 170 in 2005, and the number of articles published in the *American Psychologist* was thirty in 2006 and twenty-five in 2005, then the impact factor would be 130 + 170 (i.e. 300) divided by 30 + 25 (i.e. 55) = 5.45. Note that impact factors only cover a two-year period, and that they can change from year to year.

Table 4.2.1 shows that impact factors are not necessarily related to the circulation numbers of journals. It has been argued that a number of factors can boost impact factors. It is said that some journals gain by counting replies to articles that cite the article in question but not counting such replies as papers . . . Others suggest that authors can increase the chances of their papers being accepted by a journal if they cite other papers in that journal in their article . . . Editors can increase the impact factors of their journals by publishing more review articles, publishing good polemical articles

Table 4.2.1 Circulation numbers and impact factors for psychology journals in 2005

	Circulation	Impact factor
Behavioral and Brain Sciences	2,600	10.63
Psychological Bulletin	4,500	8.41
American Psychologist	112,000	5.49
British Journal of Psychology	2,100	1.28
The Psychologist	40,000	0.24

early in the year, and by speeding up the review process. Table 4.2.2 lists typical criticisms of impact factors.

Another weakness of impact factors is that they only measure the impact on researchers – and not on the practitioners and people who do not publish much research. The number of times an article is 'hit' or 'downloaded' might give a better indication of impact in this respect (Rowlands and Nicholas, 2007). Hit rates indicate the popularity of an article and how widely disseminated it has been, but, of course, they do not indicate if the article has been read or used. Hit rates, too, are a somewhat unreliable measure (Jacso, 2006).

In my view, which undoubtedly will be unpopular with some, authors should think first of their audience and the purpose of their communication, and put aside anything to do with impact factors – unless they have more than one suitable journal to choose between.

Table 4.2.2 Some typical criticisms of impact factors

- A journal impact factor does not necessarily reflect the quality of all of the articles in the journal.
- No correction is made for self-citations.
- Review articles are heavily referenced, and this increases the impact factor of review journals.
- Impact factors are affected by the number of articles published per year in a particular journal.
- Books are not included in calculating impact factors.
- Impact factors vary in different disciplines (and are thus not comparable). Few journals in the arts have impact factors compared with those in the sciences.
- Impact factors vary within the different sub-fields of particular disciplines.
- Small research areas tend to lack journals with high impact factors.
- High-quality research in non-English journals is rarely cited.

PUBLISHING ONLINE

In the following chapter I discuss delays in the publication process. Factors such as these can affect the choice of journal. It may well be two years or more before a submitted article finally appears in print in some journals. In these days of rapid communication, such delays are unwarrantable. So publishing your paper (or a provisional version of it) on your web site might be a sensible option.

Indeed, placing your article in an open-access national repository might be a better procedure. At the time of writing, universities and other institutions are setting up both national and local repositories to allow open access to any research materials that are produced under the aegis of the institution or research council. The UK's Joint Information Systems Committee (JISC) project 'The Depot' is an example of one such national system (see www.edina.ac.uk/news/newsline12-1/).

Another option may be to choose to publish in an open-access online journal. Open-access journals publish their papers on the Web for everyone to read, whether or not they are subscribers to the journal (although some currently charge the author over $3,000 for the privilege). Papers in online journals may also have additional features that benefit readers. For example, sometimes there are links to other papers cited in the references in an article, and to other papers on the same topic, or by the same authors. Recently, I came across one online journal, the *International Journal for the Scholarship of Teaching and Learning* (www.georgiasouthern.edu/ijsotl.) that included video clips as well as tables and figures – changing at a stroke our conceptions of what a journal should be.

Table 4.2.3 lists ten types of open-access journal. One journal, *Current Medical Research and Opinion*, for example, has two modes of rapid publication:

1   *Fast*Track, where peer review and an initial decision take two weeks from submission, and online publication is only two to three weeks from final acceptance; and
2   *Rapid*Track, where peer review and the initial decision take three to four weeks from submission, and online publication takes four to five weeks from final acceptance.

There is a production fee for papers in the *Fast*Track mode. Papers published online then subsequently appear in print four to six weeks later. *The Astrophysical Journal* has similar arrangements. Here, preprints of articles that are accepted are posted on the journal web page before the articles appear in print. As noted earlier, the editors report that papers that have appeared on the web site in this way are cited at approximately twice the rate of those that are not posted prior to publication (Schwartz and Kennicutt, 2004).

Table 4.2.3 Ten types of open access journal in 2005

Home page	University departments maintain home pages for individual faculty members on which they place their papers and make them freely available
E-print archive	An institution underwrites the hosting of repository software, enabling members to self-archive published and unpublished papers
Author fee	Author fees support immediate and complete access, and fees covered by institutional and national membership
Subsidised	Subsidy from scholarly society institution etc. enables access
Dual-mode	Subscriptions for print edition sustain both print and open-access edition
Delayed	Subscriptions for print edition and immediate open access for subscribers, with open access to all after, say, six months
Partial	Open access to a subset of articles in each edition
Charitable	Open access to students and scholars in developing countries as a charitable contribution
Indexing	Open access to bibliographic information and abstracts, often with links to pay for full texts
Co-operative	Member institutions contribute to support open access journals

Adapted from Willinsky (2005), pp. 212–13. © Massachusetts Institute of Technology, by permission of MIT Press.

Currently there appear to be four main ways of paying for publishing in an open-access journal, but the advantages and disadvantages of these (and other) methods of payment are being hotly debated at the time of writing. These four are:

- Author puts findings/paper online for free.
- Author pays to publish online in an open-access journal.
- Author's institution pays for the author to publish online in an open-access journal.
- Research funding agencies pay for publication of the research findings online in an open-access journal.

These differences are expanded upon in Table 4.2.3.

Open-access journals vary in their amount of editorial control and editing, but basically they are not so bound by the number of articles that they can print in any one issue. As noted earlier, studies suggest that self-archived papers and papers in open-access journals are cited just as, if not more, frequently on the Web than papers published in the traditional manner, but there are disputes over the reasons for this. Craig *et al.* (2007) distinguish between the following three such causes:

1   researchers are more likely to read, and thus cite, open-access articles;
2   prominent authors are more likely to make their articles available via open-access, and these will be widely read; and
3   because open-access articles appear earlier than their subsequently printed journal versions, they enjoy the benefit of this earlier appearance in the literature.

Craig *et al.* opt for this final explanation, but there is much discussion. Also, there is dispute over the suggestion that open-access can make more articles from developing countries available using these procedures (see, e.g. Antelman, 2004). Some people consider that the costs of open-access publishing for the authors or their institutions will cause greater difficulties in developing countries.

DIFFERENT AUDIENCES

Another way of disseminating your research might be to establish your name with a different audience. It is noteworthy that, since 2000, China has become the fifth leading nation in terms of its share of the world's scientific publications. Greenall (2006) describes his experiences working with publishers of school text-books in China, and Han and Zhang (2004) provide an account of the growth of psychology in China, indicating the titles of some Chinese journals in this respect. Jain (2005) presents a similar account of psychology in India. Such overseas journals may welcome reviews and articles that will reach wide audiences and be highly cited in these contexts.

REFERENCES

Antelman, K. (2004). Do open-access articles have a greater research impact? *College and Research Libraries*, 65(5), 372–82.
Craig, I. D., Plume, A. M., McVeigh, M. E., Pringle, J. & Amin, M. (2007). Do open-access articles have greater citation impact? Retrieved 12 June 2007 from *Journal of Infometrics* (www.publishingresearch.net/Citations-SummaryPaper3_000.pdf.pdf.)
Greenall, S. (2006). Made in China. *The Author*, CXVIII(3), 89–91.
Han, B. & Zhang, K. (2004). Country profile: People's Republic of China. *Psychology International*, 15(2) 8–9.
Jacso, P. (2006). Google Scholar and *The Scientist*. Retrieved 6 January 2006 from www2.hawaii.edu/~jacso/extra/gs/.
Jain, A. K. (2005). Psychology in India. *The Psychologist*, 18(4), 206–8.

Rowlands, I. & Nicholas, D. (2007). The missing link: Journal usage metrics. *ASLIB Proceedings, 59*(3), 222–8.

Schwartz, G. J. & Kennicutt, R. C. (2004). Demographics and citation trends in astrophysical journal papers and pre-prints. 10 November. Retrieved 3 September 2006 from http://arxiv.org/PS-cache/astro-ph/pdf/0411/0411275v1.pdf.

Willinsky, J. (2005). *The access principle: The case for open access to research and scholarship.* Cambridge, MA: MIT Press.

FURTHER READING

Bensman, S. J. (2007). Garfield and the impact factor. *Annual Review of Information Science and Technology, 41,* 93–155. Retrieved 3 April 2007 from http://garfield.library.upenn.edu/bensman/bensmanegif2007.pdf.

Jacobs, N. (2006). *Open access: Key strategic, technical and economic aspects.* Oxford: Chandos Publishing.

Moed, H. (2005). *Citation analysis in research evaluation.* New York: Springer.

Park, JI-H. & Qin, J. (2007). Exploring the willingness of scholars to accept open access: A grounded theory approach. *Journal of Scholarly Communication, 38*(2), 55–84.

Soloman, D. J. (2007). Medical Education Online: A case study of an open access journal in health professional education. Retrieved 15 August 2007 from *Information Research, 12*(2), paper 301 (page numbers unspecified). (http://InformationR.net/ir/12-2/paper301.html).

Delays in the publishing process

The publishers of academic journals and textbooks are notorious for what seem to the authors to be lengthy delays in the publishing process, and then announcing that the proofs will be ready in a day or two and please to have them back, corrected, within 48 hours.

If authors want to ensure rapid publication, they have to consider that certain kinds of publication are much slower than others. For example, as noted in Chapter 3.1, encyclopaedias, handbooks (with edited chapters), edited texts and conference proceedings can all take ages to emerge. Authors contributing to any one of these kinds of text can rely on someone else not to complete their contribution on time and to hold up publication. For example, when I was writing the first draft of this chapter (in August 2006), I received, out of the blue, a copy of the proofs for a conference paper that I had delivered in 2002, together with a request to return them corrected in two weeks' time . . . This does not mean that authors should not agree to write these kinds of text, but it helps if they are aware of the consequences.

DELAYS IN JOURNAL PUBLISHING

Publication lags differ in different journals. Most journals now publish with each article the dates of the original submission, the revised submission and when the article was accepted for publication – which can be a year or more before it appears in print. Researchers can get a good idea of publication delays by inspecting this information in recent issues of the journals that they intend to submit to. Generally speaking, it takes longer to publish articles in high-quality journals (often well over a year), and short notes get published more quickly than full-length articles.

New technology has been introduced into the production processes of many journals, ostensibly to aid and speed up the submission process. Certainly, such technology assists in the turnround of papers between authors, editors and referees, and it perhaps saves about twenty-five per cent of the time here (Ware, 2005), but it does not necessarily speed up the decision time taken by these different people. However, the electronic prepublication of articles considerably reduces the time it takes to make them available.

Some delays in the publication process are caused by acceptable factors – such as a large number of papers submitted, and a back-log of papers in press – but there are some unacceptable factors too. Perhaps the worst of these is the inordinate amount of time that some editors and referees take to respond. Consider these messages sent to a postgraduate student submitting one of her first papers:

1 November 2005	Manuscript submitted by post to America.
23 November 2005	Card received through post acknowledging that the manuscript had been received.
30 March 2006	Email: Please be advised that your paper submitted to X has been forwarded to me as the new editor. I should be able to advise you of a decision within a month's time. Thank you for your patience.
8 May 2006	Email sent to editor querying the status of the paper.
17 May 2006	Email: I am so sorry about the delay but it appears that several of the reviewers who were sent your ms when it was still under the editorship of X, have not replied to his request for reviews. I was able to get one review in but need at least one more. Can you send me an email copy of your paper and I will try to expedite the review process.
18 May 2006	Email: Thanks for your quick reply and for the electronic copy of your paper submitted to our journal. I think I will have another review completed within a week so we should be able to reach a decision on your paper very shortly. Thanks for your patience.
29 August 2006	Email: I hope all is well and I apologize for not getting back to you sooner. The situation with articles caught in the transition period of the journal is almost over and I am grateful for your patience. I now have the reviews for your paper (at long last). Two of the reviewers provided some very insightful recommendations that I will forward to you by surface mail. I should think that all of the points raised can be addressed in a revised paper. Please let me know if I should send the reviews to you or your co-author. I look forward to your reply.
8 September 2006	Email: 'The reviews are in the post.'
19 September 2006	Editorial decision: Accept with minor revisions.

10 October 2006	Final version of the manuscript submitted and accepted (by email).
19 December 2006	Proofs received via email.
21 May 2007	Publication date.

Similar difficulties for authors are caused by editors simply not responding. Here are the dates of messages sent to another journal:

20 May 2006	The editor dealing with papers in this section of the journal is Prof . . . at the University of . . . I am forwarding your submission to him. (Editor)
10 August 2006	(Response to a query to this section editor as to whether the submission had been received and any decision taken.) Out of office reply: I am away from the University from 1 July to 12 July and again from 15 July to 4 August.
24 August 2006	I received your manuscript but it may be a while before we can process it, because the appropriate section has only two slots per year and there is a bit of a queue at the moment.
6 November 2006	[No response to an email enquiring about progress.]
25 November 2006	Please re-submit with minor revisions.
4 December 2006	Revised manuscript submitted with query to editor about suitability of one of the changes. [No response]
26 February 2007	We are now putting the summer issue together. I have now forwarded your revised ms to my co-editors. Decisions concerning this section of the journal are taken in-house and involve three editors. We should be able to communicate an editorial decision by the end of the week. Please note that if we do decide to run it it may have to wait until the autumn edition (because there is one ms ahead of it in the queue).
3 April 2007	I'm sorry not to have come back to you earlier. The good news is that we can now proceed towards submitting your paper to the printers. Before we do, however, there are one or two smaller comments that you may want to attend to . . . (This email message was accompanied by a phone call asking if these could be done within 2 days . . .)
30 April 2007	Proofs received and corrected.
July 2007	Paper published.

Such delays are tolerable if the submissions are accepted, but, if the papers are eventually rejected or ignored, then it is hard not to feel that six months or more have been wasted.

Undoubtedly, being an editor must present problems – it must be forever like running up a downstairs escalator – for the task is never finished, but, if as an author you are expecting rapid publication, then you have been warned.

Some possible solutions to these problems are:

- Write to the editor to ask – if you have doubts – whether or not the topic/contribution of your paper is appropriate for the journal in question *before* submitting it.
- Post a copy of your article on the Web/your homepage (but beware that some journal editors might not then accept it for their print-based journals).
- Submit short notes to open-access web-based research journals, for example *Lancet's* fast track, *PubMed Central*, *Physical Review Letters* and *Psycoloquy* (as noted in Chapter 4.2).
- Post brief 'rapid responses' on the web sites of journals that accept them: for example http://bmj.com.
- Alert colleagues in appropriate web-based discussion groups of the availability of your paper (after it has been accepted for publication).
- Always have other papers 'on the go' in various stages of completion that you can work on while awaiting editors' decisions.

In addition, editors might consider reminding referees of their obligations (see Caruso and Kennedy, 2004), keeping track of their performance, or, indeed, offering payment to referees for fast performance (e.g. see *Journal of Interferon & Cytokine Research*) . . .

DELAYS IN BOOK PUBLISHING

When the contract has been signed, authors can get on with completing their text, but a number of things can hold them up. One of these, in particular, is having to obtain permission to reproduce tables, figures and quotations from previously published materials – even if they are your own originals . . .

Some people counsel authors to start doing this almost as soon as they think they will need to copy something when they set out writing their text. However, because permissions have to be given by the copyright holder (who may not always be the author), a more legal letter is required, specifying the terms and conditions of the publishers. In the case of *Academic Writing and Publishing*, for example, a letter supplied by Routledge outlined the possible print run (in hardback and paperback) and the book's likely price. It also indicated that the publisher would be seeking to produce an e-book edition and required non-exclusive English language world rights.

The publishers will supply an outline of the format for such letters – but not until the contract is signed. Then, obtaining permissions can take a long time. Routledge, for example, advise authors that obtaining permissions might take up to three months and that they cannot contemplate proceeding with the book until all the permissions have been obtained.

Some pieces may not need permission – short quotations, or prose extracts of up to 400 words, for example. Even so, it may be courteous to ask. And, indeed, all sources should be acknowledged (with page references), even if actual permission to reproduce them is not applied for.

In producing this text-book, I note that I have been held up by:

- tracing where the originals of figures I have used in the past and want to use again have come from;
- finding out that the original attribution to a source that I had in my files was wrong;
- tracing original authors' new addresses, after they have moved;
- wondering who had the copyright to a table when the original publisher had been taken over by another one, sometimes more than once;
- writing to Routledge for permission to reproduce material that I had previously published with them;
- resending requests in response to publishers' changes in their electronic processing of requests;
- rewriting to publishers and authors who did not respond to the original requests;
- revising practically all of the figure and table captions to fit the requirements of the copyright holders.

One cannot help but wonder if all of this is a charade, or an out-of-date practice. It seems to authors that publishers who push bits of paper around, and charge each other for the privilege, have not heard of open access. On the other hand, it *is* extremely irritating to see pieces of your work quoted without acknowledgement.

DELAYS IN EDITING THE TEXT

When publishers receive the author's text, it is usually submitted for copy-editing. The role of the copy-editor is to check the manuscript to ensure that it:

- follows the correct style for setting the references (in the text and in the list);

- includes all the references cited in the text in the reference list (and that there are no omissions or additions), and vice versa;
- is consistent in its punctuation for lists (such as this one);
- uses proper grammar;
- contains no typographical or spelling errors;
- reads well in terms of clarity of expression; and
- contains no obvious errors of fact or interpretation.

The copy-edited text is usually sent to the author for approval before it is finally sent to the typesetter for coding and computer-based print production.

Table 4.3.1 lists some common problems that authors should attend to before submitting a manuscript for publication.

Table 4.3.1 Some common problems that authors should attend to before submitting a manuscript

Writing	• awkward, dense or overly long sentences; • frequent repetition of the same word in a paragraph; • mixture rather than consistent use of appropriate tense; • misspellings, and inconsistencies in the spellings of authors' names; • the references contain works not included in the text, and vice versa.
Errors in APA style in the text	• text citations not in alphabetical order – (Jones, 1986: Adler, 1992) is incorrect; Adler should be first; • use of '&' in text – Jones & Johnson (1986) is not correct; it should be Jones and Johnson (1986); • use of '&' in bracketed reference – (Jones and Johnson, 1986) is incorrect; it should be (Jones & Johnston, 1986); • punctuation of 'e.g.' should be 'e.g.,'

Errors in reference lists	• Too many to mention – if done by hand rather than by computer; frequent ones include:
	  • failure to put a full stop after (Ed.), when the edited book is the only citation;
	  • failure to put a comma after (Ed.), when the reference is to a chapter in an edited book;
	  • failure to capitalise the first letter of a subtitle, after a colon;
	  • failure to give page numbers to an article in an edited book before the place and publisher, rather than after them;
	  • failure to put a space after pp. when indicating page numbers (e.g., pp. 102–5);
	  • failure to use capital letters for the keywords in a journal's title and lower-case for those in a book title;
	  • failure to include part numbers for journal references;
	  • format incorrect for signifying volume and part numbers in a journal (in the APA style, this should be 36(2) not 36 (2), or 36, 2);
	  • confusion over how to cite electronic references; the correct format is: Retrieved 20 August 2005 from www.whatever.com/. Yes, there is a full stop at the end.

Adapted from Hernon and Schwartz (2005), with permission of the authors and Elsevier Ltd.

Clearly, the more the author attends to these details in advance, the less the copy-editor has to do. Copy-editors improve the manuscript by their practised attention to detail – which most authors do not have. Copy-editors, however, might cause delays in the production process when they suggest changes that the authors disagree with, or ask them to write more text.

Copy-editors have a more difficult task when they are dealing with translated books or papers, or when authors are writing in their second language. Here, the copy-editor has to consider the appropriateness of individual words, rewriting individual sentences and, possibly, whole paragraphs (see Misak et al., 2005; Shashok and Kerans, 2000).

I expressed the view in Chapter 1.1 that, with new technology, it was now harder to detect changes in an author's manuscript than it was before. This may be true, but research on copy-editing has begun to focus on the changes that copy-editors make to the finally submitted manuscripts. Wates and Campbell (2007), for instance, examined the changes made to 189 research articles taken from a mixture of journals in the sciences, social sciences and the humanities. Five kinds of change were recorded:

- the copy-editors' suggestions for typographical changes on the proofs;
- the copy-editors' suggestions for more substantial changes on the proofs;
- the number of changes made by the author in response to these;
- the number of suggestions ignored by the author; and
- the number of additional changes made by the author.

The results showed that, on average, there were nine queries per article, and authors responded to 8.4 of these, which left 0.6 (on average) ignored or unanswered. Forty-three per cent of the queries related to the accuracy of the references, thirty-five per cent to minor syntactical or grammatical errors, fourteen per cent to missing data, six per cent to correcting errors that might have led to misunderstandings or misinterpretations, and four per cent to appropriate terminology for units of measurement. Wates and Campbell (2007) concluded that copy editors were doing a valuable job and that none of the changes that they suggested materially altered the conclusions of the articles in question. This, however, was not the conclusion of Goodman et al. (2007).

Goodman et al. compared twenty-four authors' manuscripts placed on open access (after peer review) with their edited versions that finally appeared in print. Twelve of these articles were from journals in the social sciences, and twelve from the field of biochemistry. Comparisons were made between three main levels of assessment:

1   errors that would be normally adjusted by proof reading or minor copy-editing;

2   omissions that copy-editors would not necessarily be able to correct; and
3   severe differences (in the data or the conclusions) which could lead two readers, each with a different version, to draw different conclusions.

The researchers found that seven of the twelve social science articles presented no problems above level 1, but that, for the other five, three were more detailed in the authors' online versions than in the printed ones, and two were the reverse of this, omitting details that were necessary to evaluate the validity of the conclusions. Better results were found with the biochemistry articles. Here, eight provided no problems above level 1, two of the published versions were slightly improved by the editing process, and two were substantially improved in this respect.

Goodman *et al.* concluded that, in the context of open-access publishing, there might sometimes be copy-edited changes to open-access papers that could lead to errors in the finally printed versions although, in most cases, the changes led to improvements.

REFERENCES

Caruso, M. & Kennedy, H. (2004). Effects of a reviewer prompting strategy on timely manuscript reviews. *Journal of Applied Behavior Analysis*, *37*(4), 523–6.

Goodman, D., Dowson, S. & Yaremchuk, J. (2007). Open access and accuracy: Author-archived manuscripts vs. published articles. *Learned Publishing*, *20*(3), 203–15.

Hernon, P. & Schwartz, C. (2005). The unsung hero to a high-quality peer review journal. *Library & Information Science Research*, *27*(4), 421–3.

Misak, A., Marusic, M. & Marusic, A. (2005). Manuscript editing as a way of teaching academic writing: Experience from a small scientific journal. *Journal of Second Language Writing*, *14*(2), 122–31.

Shashok, K. & Kerans, M. E. (2000). Translating the unedited science manuscript: Who fixes what shortcomings? In J. Chabas, M. Cases & R. Glaser (Eds.), *Proceedings: 1st international conference on specialized translation* (pp. 101–4). Barcelona: Universitat Pompeu Fabra.

Ware, M. (2005). *Online submission and peer review systems*. Worthing: Association of Learned and Professional Society Publishers.

Wates, E. & Campbell, R. (2007). Author's version vs. publisher's version: An analysis of the copy-editing function. *Learned Publishing*, *20*(2) 121–9.

Chapter 4.4

Refereeing

In 2006, the editor of the *British Journal of Educational Technology* emailed his panel of over 150 referees to ask them if they were happy with the procedures used to referee articles submitted to his journal. In this case, the referees choose papers that they would like to referee from an electronic menu. They make their selection from the editor's list, which gives them the names of the authors and the titles of the submitted publications. The referees review the paper and send their reports via the editor to the author, unsigned. This process is called a 'single-blind review'. In a 'double-blind review', the names of the authors and their institutions are deleted from the manuscripts, and the referees do not sign their reports. (Two other possibilities exist: 'open review' – where both the authors and the referees names are known to each other, and another (rare) form of single-blind review – where the referee's name is known to the authors, but their names are not known to the referee.)

There were some two dozen replies to the editor's question. Most of these supported the editor's approach, some others were more neutral and raised additional concerns, and only three supported double-blind refereeing. These responses suggest that there was no serious opposition to the notion that referees should get to see the name(s) of the authors in advance, but that they should not give their names when refereeing the papers – a rather self-indulgent position.

But what does the research say about the strengths and limitations of these different procedures? There have been several studies of blind reviewing detailing its advantages and disadvantages. Weller (2001) provides a useful, if now somewhat dated, summary. It appears that:

1   referees can usually detect correctly the name of a deleted author about forty per cent of the time;
2   there appears to be little difference in the rejection rates of papers refereed blind or not;
3   the language used in open referees' reports differs little from that used in blind ones; and
4   there is little evidence for any gender bias in the refereeing of journal articles.

'Peer review' is the general name given to this process, where articles are submitted to a journal editor and are then sent out to two, three or more colleagues for review. These colleagues make recommendations, and the editor then decides whether or not to accept or reject the paper. Rejection rates vary across and within disciplines. Thus, eighty per cent of submissions in the social sciences are typically rejected, whereas this figure is typically twenty-five per cent in the sciences.

Normally, when asked to referee a paper, the referees have to:

1   fill out an evaluation form;
2   make an overall recommendation;
3   provide comments for the author(s) supporting their judgements; and
4   provide comments for the editor(s) supporting their judgements.

Actions 1, 2 and 3 are usually done anonymously, and copies of 2 and 3 are sent by the editor to the author(s), together with the decision letter.

EVALUATION FORMS

Figure 4.4.1 shows one such evaluation form. This form is fairly typical, but different journals use different forms, and some ask referees to rate more features than do others.

All of these forms, however, require the referee to make *one* of the following overall recommendations to the editor:

- accept for publication;
- accept with minor revisions;
- consider a resubmission after major revisions have been made in the light of the referees' comments (the editor alone might consider the resubmission, or the revised paper might be sent back to the original referees for further comments, or even to different referees);
- reject.

Editors consider the evaluation forms received from (usually) two or three referees and then decide what to do next on the basis of their recommendations (and their own reading of the paper).

COMMENTS TO THE AUTHOR(S)

As noted earlier, referees are not always consistent in what they recommend. Different referees have different opinions, and there has been much research on the reliability and validity of peer review systems (e.g. see Godlee and

Please rate the paper as follows:

	GOOD	AVERAGE	POOR
Strength of supporting data/evidence	_____	_____	_____
Originality of ideas and approach	_____	_____	_____
Significance of topic	_____	_____	_____
Completeness of discussion	_____	_____	_____
Quality of writing	_____	_____	_____
Intelligibility to non-specialists	_____	_____	_____

RECOMMENDATION

Accept _____   Accept with minor revisions _____

Re-submit after major revision _____   Reject _____

COMMENTS
Please add any comments for the editor here:

COMMENTS FOR THE AUTHOR(S)
Please type comments for the authors on a separate page

Figure 4.4.1 A typical evaluation sheet for editors and referees.

Jefferson, 2003; Hojat *et al.*, 2003; Weller, 2001). Weller, for example, reviewed over thirty studies on the topic and concluded that they indicated that there was not a lot of agreement between referees. She also suggested, however, that agreement between referees about whether or not a paper should be rejected was usually higher than it was about whether or not a paper should be accepted.

There are few personal accounts in the literature of how different referees go about the process of refereeing but the ones that have been published are instructive (see, e.g. Benos *et al.*, 2003; Hoppin, 2002; Lee, 1995). Here I describe my own procedures in this respect.

First of all, I download the paper for review and then I read it twice – trying hard not to scribble any comments on it on the first reading. This preliminary reading allows me to think about the overall recommendations I shall be making on the evaluation scale, the opening paragraph of my comments to the author(s), and any comments that I might make privately to the editor.

Next, I read the paper again, making specific notes/comments/queries to myself on the actual text, paragraph by paragraph and even line by line.

Then, I word-process a general set of opening remarks for the author(s), trying to be positive, and indicating what my general recommendations will be. Here, I typically summarise the purpose of the paper (to help the editor remember what is was about) and I might indicate my expertise – or lack of it – with respect to certain parts of the paper. I head these comments 'General remarks'.

Next, I list, in sequence and by appropriate page number, paragraph or line, any specific comments I might have (under the heading 'Specific comments'). Making these comments sometimes helps me to clarify or add to the general remarks written above. Finally, I have a third section 'Minor points' – where I might note an occasional ungrammatical sentence, a reference that is cited in the text but not in the reference list, and a correction to a date of publication etc. I do not usually bother with these minor points if I feel the paper should be rewritten or rejected.

As noted above, I list my specific comments and minor points in page sequence (and not in order of importance). I do this simply to help me and the authors locate the focus of my remarks. The kinds of comments I typically make are:

- suggestions for improving the clarity of the title/abstract;
- queries about the procedures, the data and inferences;
- wondering about the need for additional or more appropriate statistics;
- implying the necessity for additional/updated references; and
- requesting more detail and/or clearer explanations, etc.

Table 4.4.1 lists the more general concerns of referees. Information such as this may be instructive for new referees. Godoy (2006), in an interesting paper, describes how a group of young faculty members in engineering benefited from comparing their reviews with those written by more experienced colleagues.

GENERAL ADVICE

Some points to bear in mind, when writing both general and specific comments, are as follows:

- Be courteous throughout. There is no need to be superior, sarcastic or to show off. Remember the paper that you are refereeing might have been written by a postgraduate, and it could be a first attempt at publication.

Table 4.4.1 The main concerns of referees (adapted with permission from Brown (2004) courtesy of *The Scientist* and *Sense about Science*, www.senseaboutscience. org)

Significance	Are the findings original? Are they important? Is the paper suitable for this journal? Does the article justify its length?
Scholarship	Does the paper take into account relevant current and past research on the topic?
Presentation	Is the paper clear, logical, understandable and of the appropriate length?
Methods and results	Is the methodology, and are the data and analyses appropriate? Are there sufficient data to support the conclusion? Are there long-term as well as short-term measures? Are any weaknesses of the method commented on?
Reasoning	Are the logic, arguments, inferences and interpretations appropriate? Are counter-arguments or contrary evidence taken into account and discussed?
Theory	Is the theory sufficiently sound and supported by the evidence? Is it testable? Is it preferable to competing theories?
Ethics	In papers describing work on animals or humans, has the work been approved by the appropriate ethics committee?

- Avoid criticising the paper because it does not do what you might have done. Judge it on its own merits.
- Explain any criticisms that you make. There must always be a reason for them. This will help the author(s) to respond to any criticisms (or not) when they are resubmitting.
- Remember that papers from overseas authors can be a special case. Here, if there are difficulties in the writing, you will have to concentrate initially on the content and not let such difficulties cloud your judgement. If you think that the paper is interesting and worthwhile, then you might either make suggestions then and there about the writing, or indicate to the editor that the paper might require careful copy-editing at a later date, if it is accepted.
- Try to help the author(s) to improve the paper. If the authors are, say, American and they include no references to relevant British work (or vice versa) it might be helpful to say so – and to give one or two *easily accessible* references. If you do suggest the need for additional references, always give the full citations. Nothing is more infuriating for an author than to be told by a referee that you have omitted key studies but not to be told what they are!
- Complete your report as quickly as you can, but do not rush it. The editor will be indebted to you if you respond promptly, and so will the

author(s). It is appalling how long some referees take to do the job. Indeed, as noted in Chapter 4.3, to counter this, the *Journal of Interferon & Cytokine Research* has started to pay its referees for speedy replies.

- Keep the content of the manuscript and your report confidential, and do not cite such privileged information in anything that you are writing.

Clearly, there is no one way to referee a paper. Referees will find it instructive to receive from the editor, at a later date, copies of the comments written by the other referees about the same paper. They might be surprised by the differences between the reports. Some points will be shared, but others will be individual.

HOW OFTEN ARE PEOPLE ASKED TO REFEREE?

Different editors have different conceptions of how many papers referees might reasonably be asked to do. Some argue that, as each paper needs about three referees, including the editor, an author might be expected to referee two papers for every one that they submit. Others think that editors should not try to overwork referees and, therefore, do not ask them to do more than, say, two papers per year. These editors, though, tend to forget that referees might referee for more than one journal. Refereeing is thus a bit like writing papers: some do a lot, some do very little.

WHAT DO WRITERS GAIN BY REFEREEING?

Commentators suggest that writers gain three things by refereeing:

1   they feel accepted as part of the scholarly community;
2   they have to take a stand and decide what is and what is not acceptable in publications in their discipline; and
3   they see the level of quality demanded of other authors and learn to apply it to their own work.

Refereeing a paper conscientiously is time-consuming but worthwhile. It may take several hours to do it properly. Many authors acknowledge the contribution of referees to their publications, and some studies have shown that papers revised after refereeing are judged to be of higher quality than were their original versions (Godlee and Jefferson, 2003; Weller, 2001). Refereeing is thus part of quality control in the publication process. As Weller (2001) says, 'editorial peer review is messy and does not always work as it should' (p. 322). Nonetheless, it is probably better to read a refereed paper than the original submission. Making the original submission better is where referees come in.

REFEREEING OTHER GENRES

Finally, we should note that books, book chapters and applications for research funding are also subject to refereeing.

Books

When authors submit proposals for books to publishers (see Chapter 3.1), it is usual for these publishers to send out the proposals to two or three referees for comment. These referees may have been nominated by the author, they may be chosen by the publishers, or they may be a mixture of both. Publishers require honest answers to the following kinds of question (Vandenbos *et al.*, 2006):

- Does the plan for the proposed volume appear sound?
- Is the projected content comprehensive, appropriate and timely?
- Are the suggested chapters appropriately focused? Should any chapters be added or deleted?
- Do the chapters provide strong theoretical and empirical support?
- Does the proposed text represent current scientific and professional knowledge in a balanced way?
- Do you believe that there is a need as well as a market for the proposed book?

The assessors are being thus being asked about biases, the author's judgements, and whether or not the book will sell. These questions are typically asked of all the publisher's books in a standard questionnaire to be completed by the assessors.

Book chapters

The refereeing process here is quite different from that used for refereeing papers. Chapters that have been submitted for publication in an edited collection are likely to be longer and written by an authority in the field. The task of the referee here is typically to identify the good points in the chapter and perhaps the weaker ones, and to indicate how things might be improved. Comments may be asked for on the length of the chapter and the coverage of the literature review: Is it up to date? Has anything been missed out? Is it too long? The general aim here is to judge if the content is appropriate and perhaps suggest some possible improvements.

Research and grant proposals

The refereeing process here is more like refereeing papers, but it is a good deal more demanding. A great deal is at stake when one recommends acceptance or rejection of a research proposal costing several thousands of pounds. Referees in this context have to be authorities in the field, and they should possibly decline to do the task if they think they are not. Gade *et al.* (2006) indicate that the reviewer's report has to be thorough, clear, specific, constructive and timely. Referees are typically asked to assess, often with rating scales, the quality of the proposal, the appropriateness of the time-scale for the research, the costs involved and the competence of the researchers to carry it out. Often, an overall grading is required: A++ = well above average; A= above average; B = good etc. Refereeing a grant proposal is not easy, and not all A++ proposals get funded. Furthermore, there is evidence here of gender bias in favour of men (Bornmann *et al.*, 2007).

REFERENCES

Benos, J., Kirk, K. K. & Hall, J. E. (2003). How to review a paper. *Advances in Physiology Education, 27*(2), 47–52.

Bornmann, L., Mutz, R. & Daniel, H-D. (2007). Gender differences in grant peer review: A meta-analysis. *Journal of Informetrics, 1*, 226–38.

Brown, T. (2004). Stop whispering about peer review. *The Scientist, 18*(17), 8–9.

Gade, P. A., Constanza, D. P. & Kaplan, J. D. (2006). Reviewing grant and contract proposals. In R. J. Sternberg (Ed.), *Reviewing scientific works in psychology* (pp. 101–23). Washington: American Psychological Association.

Godlee, F. & Jefferson, T. (Eds.) (2003). *Peer review in health sciences* (2nd edn). London: BMJ Publishing Group.

Godoy, L. A. (2006). Differences between experts and novices in the review of engineering papers. *Journal of Professional Issues in Engineering Education and Practice, 132*(1), 24–8.

Hojat, J. S., Gonnella, J. S. & Caelleigh, A. S. (2003). Impartial judgement by the 'gatekeepers' of science: Fallibility and accountability in the peer review process. *Advances in Health Sciences Education, 8*(1), 75–96.

Hoppin, F. G. (2002). How I review an original scientific article. *American Journal of Respiratory and Critical Care Medicine, 166*(8), 1019–23.

Lee, A. S. (1995). Reviewing a manuscript for publication. *Journal of Operations Management, 13*(1), 87–92.

VandenBos, G. R., Frank-McNeil, J. & Amsel, J. (2006). Reviewing book proposals. In R. J. Sternberg (Ed.), *Reviewing scientific works in psychology* (pp. 79–88). Washington: American Psychological Association.

Weller, A. C. (2001). *Editorial peer review: Its strengths and weaknesses.* Medford, NJ: Information Today.

FURTHER READING

Eisenberg, N., Thompson, M. S., Augir, S. & Stanley, E. H. (2002). 'Getting in' revisited: An analysis of manuscript characteristics, reviewers' ratings, and acceptance of manuscripts in *Psychological Bulletin*. *Psychological Bulletin*, *128*(6), 997–1004.

Gosden, H. (2003). 'Why not give us the full story?': Functions of referees' comments in peer reviews of scientific research papers. *Journal of English for Academic Purposes*, *2*(2), 87–101.

Kumashiro, K. K. (2005). Thinking collaboratively about the review process for journal article publication. *Harvard Educational Review*, *75*(3), 257–85.

Lounds, J., Oakar, M., Knecht, K., Moran, M., Gibney, M. & Pressly, M. (2002). Journal editors' views on the criteria a paper must meet to be publishable. *Contemporary Educational Psychology*, *27*(2), 338–47.

Spector, P. E. (1998). When reviewers become authors: A comment on the journal review process. Retrieved 19 September 2006 from http:division.aomonline.org/rm1998_forum_reviewers_become_authors.html.

Sternberg, R. J. (Ed). (2006). *Reviewing scientific works in psychology*. Washington, DC: American Psychological Association.

Sex differences in academic writing

In Chapter 1.1 I discussed some differences between the writing processes of individual academics. In that chapter, I did not report, nor indeed have I found, any data on sex differences in this respect. This is surprising given that there has always been an interest in differences between the sexes in terms of verbal ability.

It is commonly held that women are more verbal than men. Consequently, there is considerable discussion about whether or not men and women write and speak in different ways. In a major review of the field, Pennebaker *et al.* (2003) concluded that women, in general, use more words related to psychological and social processes, and that men refer more to object properties and impersonal topics. However, these conclusions, of course, are related to the topics that men and women speak and write about, and how salient these topics are for them. Men and women, when they are talking about specifically masculine and feminine things (e.g. football and cosmetics), do differ in their spoken language, but do they differ in how they write about them?

STUDENTS WRITING IN HIGHER EDUCATION

A number of studies have looked to see whether or not male students write differently from female students in English university examinations. Here, there are two particular genres: course-work essays done over time, and essay-examination scripts done under pressure of time. The findings for either genre are not particularly convincing. Studies in both situations have found that women do better than men in some situations, and men do better than women in others, but in both genres there seem to be more similarities than differences (Hartley *et al.*, 2007). The majority of these studies have involved small sample sizes and used examination *marks* as the criteria for concluding that men do better than women or vice versa. Nonetheless, one aspect sometimes discussed in this context is whether or not men are more assertive in their examination essays than women (e.g. Robson *et al.*, 2002). In these studies, the *wording* of the essays has to be examined.

Here, the approach taken has been to examine essays for differences between men and women on various selected measures (e.g. emotional words, numbers, personal pronouns, etc.). Usually, this has been done by counting these features by hand for the different sexes. Such complexities tend to reduce both the numbers of students and essays involved, and the lengths of the texts that are sampled. In addition, different authors have selected different features to discriminate between the writings of men and women, so that the results of the studies are not always comparable.

Today, however, computer-based counting measures can be used. These newer techniques, using much larger samples and a greater variety of measures, allow one to look more quickly and more reliably for differences between the writings of men and women. As noted in Chapter 1.1, the computer program *Linguistic Inquiry and Word Count* (LIWC) for example, calculates the percentage of words used in any one text in any one of seventy-four different linguistic categories. Furthermore, again as noted in Chapter 1.1, some of these separate categories can be grouped – for example, into emotional words (e.g. 'happy', 'sad', 'angry'), self-references (e.g. 'I', 'we') and cognitive words (e.g. 'realise', 'think', 'understand'). Unfortunately, LIWC has not been used in many studies of academic text, although there have been some (e.g. Hartley *et al.*, 2002; Hartley *et al.*, 2003; Rude *et al.*, 2004). Again, few sex differences have been found in these studies.

EMAIL STUDIES

Investigators have, however, reported more success in using new technology to assess differences between the language of male and female students using email. Here, it is claimed, it is possible to detect whether or not a student's email has been written by a man or a woman by examining the language that is used (Colley *et al.*, 2004; Thomson and Murachver, 2001). Colley *et al.*, for instance, found that female students' emails were longer than those of men, used less offensive language, and contained more humour and exclamation marks when they were sent to other women.

ACADEMIC WRITING

Returning to fully fledged academics, there have been few studies of sex differences in the writings of academics, and thus there are fewer findings to report. In one complex study, using LIWC, we only found minor differences when we compared academic articles written by individual and pairs of men with those written by individual and pairs of women (Hartley *et al.*, 2003). The clearest difference, which we could not explain, was that single men and pairs of women produced texts with higher readability scores than did pairs of men and single women!

WRITING AS A GENRE

Table 4.5.1 shows some data found for men and women writing in different genres, ranging from academic text to what is often called 'women's fiction'. If you read *down* the table, for both of the measures 'sentence length' and 'reading ease', you will see that the texts typically get easier the further you go down the columns. If you read *across* the columns, you will find that there is only one significant difference out of eighteen between the average scores achieved by men and women. Basically, the data in Table 4.5.1 show

Table 4.5.1 Mean scores (and standard deviations) for men and women authors on measures of readability for different text genres

Genre	Sentence lengths (in words)		% of passive sentences		Flesch RE score*	
	Men	Women	Men	Women	Men	Women
1 Academic book reviews						
Mean	28.0	26.2	8.9	8.3	21.4	24.5
(s.d.)	8.0	5.1	8.5	11.3	9.8	10.6
N=30 for each sex						
2 Academic articles						
Mean	25.8	25.5	20.9	19.0	20.2	24.8
(s.d.)	4.2	4.7	10.6	11.6	8.9	9.2
N=19 for each sex						
3 Student essays						
Mean	26.2	25.3	31.0	26.9	31.8	27.3
(s.d)	3.3	3.8	15.4	14.5	8.0	10.5
N=15 for each sex						
4 Tabloid newspaper articles						
Mean	21.0	21.7	14.8	22.7**	52.5	54.5
(s.d.)	2.4	4.8	7.5	7.8	6.3	7.9
N=10 for each sex						
5 Novels						
Mean	17.5	16.9	6.1	4.3	68.8	74.9
(s.d.)	7.8	6.1	7.3	4.0	11.2	8.6
N=10 for each sex						
6 Magazine fiction						
Mean	12.7	12.0	3.1	2.6	79.9	78.7
(s.d.)	3.4	2.7	3.1	2.0	5.7	5.8
N=10 for each sex						

* Flesch RE scores range from 0 to 100, with easier texts having higher scores (as shown here). Texts with scores below 30 are labelled 'very difficult'
** This difference between the use of passives is statistically significant (t = 2.18, d.f. 18, p<.05). It is the only significant difference in this table and thus it could have occurred by chance
Updated from Hartley (2005).

that men and women write equally well in any genre, but that these genres can differ markedly from each other.

One interesting possibility to consider here is that the more complex text in Table 4.5.1 is typically labelled 'masculine' (as academic and legal text was originally written by men), and that the less complex text is typically labelled 'feminine' (as this type of fiction is written more frequently by women). Whatever the case, when we turn to academic writing, it is clear – from these measures – that academic writing:

1   has a complex style
2   is difficult to read
3   can be performed equally well by men and women.

REFERENCES

Colley, A., Todd, Z., Bland, M., Holmes, M., Khanon, R. & Pike, H. (2004). Style and content in emails and letters to male and female friends. *Journal of Language and Social Psychology, 23*(3), 369–78.

Hartley, J. (2005). Is academic writing masculine? *Higher Education Review, 37*(2), 53–62.

Hartley, J., Betts, L. J. & Murray, W. (2007). Gender and assessment: Differences, similarities and implications. *Psychology Teaching Review, 13*(1), 34–47.

Hartley, J., Pennebaker, J. W. & Fox, C. (2003). Using new technology to assess the academic writing styles of male and female pairs and individuals. *Journal of Technical Writing and Communication, 33*(3), 243–61.

Hartley, J., Sotto, E. & Pennebaker, J, W. (2002). Style and substance in psychology: Are influential papers more readable than less influential ones? *Social Studies of Science, 32*(2), 321–34.

Pennebaker, J. W., Mehl, M. R. & Niederhoffer, K. (2003). Psychological aspects of natural language use: Our words, our selves. *Annual Review of Psychology, 54*, 547–77.

Robson, J., Francis, B. & Read, B. (2002). Writes of passage: Stylistic features of male and female undergraduate history essays. *Journal of Further and Higher Education, 26*(4), 351–62.

Rude, S.S., Gortner, E-M. & Pennebaker, J. W. (2004). Language use of depressed and depression-vulnerable college students. *Cognition and Emotion, 18*(8), 1121–33.

Thompson, R. & Murachver, T. (2001). Predicting gender from electronic discourse. *British Journal of Social Psychology, 40*(2), 193–208.

FURTHER READING

Fox, M. F. (2005). Gender, family characteristics, and publication productivity among scientists. *Social Studies of Science, 35*(1), 131–50.

Martin, M. (1997). Emotional and cognitive effects of examination proximity in female and male students. *Oxford Review of Education, 23*(4), 479–86.

Peterson, S. (2006). Influence of gender on writing development. In C. A. MacArthur, S. Graham & J. Fitzgerald (Eds.). *Handbook of writing research* (pp. 311–23). New York: Guilford.

Procrastination and writer's block

As noted in Chapter 1.1, the texts that we read do not display individual differences in the approaches of their authors. Nor do they show how different writers feel about writing. Texts may be written with gusto and joy, or with painstaking agony, but this is not apparent from their surface features. Madigan *et al.* (1996) show this in their study. Here, the essays of psychology students were grouped into three categories (with about thirty essays in each). These were written by students with high, medium or low anxiety about writing. Then, the essays of the high and the low groups were compared. The investigators were unable to find any significant differences in their quality as measured by various measures of syntactic complexity. What they did find, however, from questioning the students at the end of the essay writing session, was that the students who were generally anxious about writing:

1 tended to make more negative comments to themselves as they were writing; and
2 generally viewed writing as an unpleasant and unrewarding activity.

From this, we might well ask how far do feelings such as these slow down or actually prevent writing from occurring?

PROCRASTINATION

One way of avoiding unpleasant tasks is to put off doing them – or to procrastinate. I am not sure that it is helpful to list all of the ways of procrastinating that I can think of, but Table 4.6.1 includes some obvious ones. The trick here, I suppose, is to learn to recognise that these activities are *distractors*, and then to allow yourself the luxury of doing them – well, some of them – as a reward, *after* completing some writing.

Table 4.6.1 Things that writers do to avoid writing . . .

At home
- washing up, dusting, vacuuming, doing the laundry, drinking coffee, reading the papers, gardening, decorating, etc.

In the office
- checking emails, tidying the office, sorting papers, looking for a particular paper, re-filing papers, going for coffee with colleagues, creating new folders on the computer, emailing old friends, working on a different paper, etc.

WRITER'S BLOCK

It is a short step from writing apprehension and procrastination to writer's block – 'a temporary or chronic inability to put words on paper' (Nelson, 1993, p. 1). In its extreme case, this means that nothing gets written for a week or two, a month or two, or even a year or two. Writers in this situation often complain that the task is too complex, that they have too much conflicting material to deal with, and that the task is just too big. Problems such as these make them depressed, their initial enthusiasm disappears, and they feel inadequate and not up to the job (see Table 4.6.2).

Most studies of procrastination and writer's block have been conducted with students. There is, however, some literature relating to researchers and academics. Silvia (2007), in a surprisingly short book, given its title, *How to Write a Lot*, provides some practical advice, and Boice (1990) provides a more detailed treatment. Silvia and Boice discuss the following factors in writer's block:

- procrastination
- fear of failure
- self-censoring criticism
- perfectionism

Table 4.6.2 Quotations on procrastination from academic writers

I don't know where to go next. Sometimes I just give up and do something else . . . Other times I just try to write my way through it, knowing that I'll probably delete most of it.

It is a struggle, it's a real struggle. You are laying yourself bare: what will people think about it? That can mean that you get completely stuck and not want to write.

Reading is a good way of filling in time and not starting to write.

I get [writer's block] all the time and I don't deal with it. I just stay there and plug away.

Reproduced from Wellington (2003), pp. 31–5 with permission of the author and the publishers.

- time pressure
- personality factors and mood disorders.

Boice includes a questionnaire in his text and he uses the patterns of responses to questions on these different features to prescribe personally tailored methods for overcoming an individual writer's block. More generally, Silvia and Boice's solutions to handling these problems lie in:

1   rearranging the writer's environment
2   rearranging the writer's writing habits.

To rearrange the writing environment, they suggest that writers should:

- establish one or a *few* regular places in which to work
- minimise distractions
- limit social interruptions.

To rearrange writing habits, they suggest that writers should:

- make writing a daily activity;
- write while fresh;
- write in small, regular amounts, and avoid 'binge sessions';
- schedule writing tasks in small sizes in order to keep up;
- capitalise on post-writing thinking: here, one might jot down issues or make notes on the back of an envelope, use a mini dictating machine, or even phone or text ideas home to a message machine; and
- share their writing with supportive, constructive friends.

Some other practical suggestions that help some people to get started are as follows:

- Make time to write: if possible, set aside a specific time for writing each day.
- Recognise and label distractors as distractors, and ignore them.
- Do not aim for perfection on the first draft. Let it flow, and then come back to polish it.
- Start by reading what you have produced so far, and spend a bit of time rephrasing things, clarifying or adding in a reference or quotation.
- Make a note of the structure of the text you want to write – and list its main headings. Then work to these, perhaps one at a time, and not necessarily in order.
- Do not stop writing at the end of a section. Write one or two sentences of the next one and then finish. Pick up from where you left off when you next begin.

- Do not finish the end of a section by running the spell and grammar checker before you switch off. You can do this the next time you begin.
- Do not stop to correct and revise. Keep going and then come back to do this later.
- Reward yourself for meeting your targets.

REFERENCES

Boice, R. (1990). *Professors as writers: A self-help guide to productive writing*. Stillwater, OK: New Forums Press.

Madigan, R., Linton, P. & Johnson, S. (1996). The paradox of writing apprehension. In C. M. Levy & S. Ransdell (Eds.), *The science of writing: Theories, methods, individual differences and applications* (pp. 295–307). Mahwah, NJ: Erlbaum.

Nelson, V. (1993). *On writers' block: A new approach to creativity*. New York: Houghton Mifflin.

Silvia, P. J. (2007). *How to write a lot: A practical guide to productive academic writing*. Washington, DC: American Psychological Association.

Wellington, J. (2003). *Getting published: A guide for lecturers and researchers*. London: Routledge.

FURTHER READING

Ferrari, J. R. (2001). Getting things done on time: Conquering procrastination. In C. R. Snyder (Ed.), *Coping with stress: Effective people and processes* (pp. 30–46). Oxford: Oxford University Press.

Collaborative writing

The number of authors who collaborate has been steadily rising over the years, although there are disciplinary variations (Lewison and Hartley, 2005). Collaboration has been highest among scientists and lowest among arts specialists. International collaboration – as measured by co-authorships on papers in the sciences – has also grown significantly (Abt, 2007).

The literature in this area suggests that collaborative writing among academics can:

1   be more efficient – because different aspects of the task can be shared out;
2   be of better quality – because different individuals can contribute different expertise; and
3   lead to better written papers – because each individual contributor can assist in the writing and the editing of the paper, each seeing it from different perspectives.

Bahr and Zemon (2000) discuss some of the evidence used to arrive at these conclusions. They cite studies showing that:

(i)   single authors in librarianship submit more papers, but that papers by multiple authors are published more frequently;
(ii)   papers by multiple authors require less revision; and
(iii) papers by multiple authors receive more citations.

More recently, in a survey of 443 physical scientists, natural scientists and engineers, Lee and Bozerman (2005) found a strong correlation between collaborative activity and research productivity when just the number of papers were counted. However, when the number of papers were adjusted for the number of authors, then the specific number of collaborators was not a significant predictor of productivity. Other studies in other contexts have provided different results. For example, Duque *et al.* (2005) did not find correlations between collaboration and productivity in their study of scientists in Ghana, Kenya and the state of Kerala in south-west India. Wigg *et al.* (2006) only found small but positive correlations between the numbers of authors and subsequent citation rates in six biomedical journals that had high impact factors. Indeed, in this particular study, the picture differed slightly in each journal, so that it was not possible to pool the data to present a clear conclusion.

There are other, perhaps more unexpected findings from studies of co-authorship. Thus, for example, Lewison and Hartley (2005) reported that:

1   the more authors there were, the longer (on average) were the titles of their paper;
2   the more authors there were, the longer (on average) was the paper itself; and
3   single authors used colons in their titles significantly more than did pairs or groups of authors (until the number of authors reached twelve or more)!

DIFFERENT WAYS OF COLLABORATING

Sharples (1999) describes three main ways of proceeding with multiple authorship: parallel, sequential and reciprocal. *Parallel working* is the classic 'division of labour', where a job is divided up among the workers into sub-tasks. Different people do different jobs. *Sequential working* is like a production line. The first person hands on the part-completed topic for the next one to continue. *Reciprocal working* is the way a football or basketball team operates. All the partners work together, mutually adjusting their activities to take account of each other's contributions.

However, these descriptions do not match (in my experience) the methods used by most joint authors of academic papers in the social sciences. Sharples' descriptions fit better with notions of hierarchy and power in a scientific laboratory. Writers of social science papers are more likely to maintain a collegiate or 'dialogic' form of collaboration, so that colleagues are often equal partners in the enterprise. Here, there are several possibilities for pairs of writers, as shown in Table 4.7.1, ranging from Level 1 – no collaboration – to Level 4 – high collaboration. Sometimes, this collaboration is intensive, when two or more collaborators work closely together on a single text, and sometimes it is less intensive, when authors might collaborate together at times and work on the paper separately at others. Lee and Bozerman (2005) usefully distinguish in this context between the number of collaborators (which can be large or small) and the number of collaborations between them (which can be high or low).

Table 4.7.2 compares the advantages and disadvantages of working in pairs, listed by educational research psychologists. These separate roles, of

Table 4.7.1 Different kinds of collaboration when writing in pairs described by 28 educational psychologists

1.	No collaboration First author writes it all		
2a	First author writes all Second author comments First author revises the whole	2b	First author writes some parts Second author writes other parts First author revises the whole
3a	First author writes all Second author comments First author revises the whole Second author comments First author revises the whole	3b	First author writes some parts Second author writes other parts Both authors comment First author revises the whole
4a	As above, but multiple exchanges until both authors are satisfied	4b	As above, but multiple exchanges until both authors are satisfied

Note: Authors also vary in their ways of collaboration according to who they collaborate with, and the topics on which they are writing.

Reproduced with permission from Hartley *et al.* (2003), p. 256. © Baywood Publishing Company.

course, are merging. The advent of new technology has meant that it is now easier to exchange drafts of manuscripts and to work on them together (see Chapter 4.8). As noted in Chapter 2.2, the APA *Publication Manual* (2001) gives clear advice on the last point in Table 4.7.2 (allocating credit for authorship).

Table 4.7.2 The advantages and disadvantages of writing in pairs

Advantages

Each serves as an editor for the other.
One person may have different psychological skills from the other, which can then be pooled.
One person may have different subject matter expertise from the other, which can lead to the research being done in the first place.
Writing in pairs provides training for student co-authors.

Disadvantages

Problems arise if colleagues don't get on well together.
Production can be slowed down if one colleague has too many other things to do.
It is more of an effort for the first author if he or she is working with a student.
It is more of an effort for the first author if the colleague's work is insufficient/ inadequate (and vice versa).
There may be potential hassles over who will be designated as first author.

Reproduced with permission from Hartley *et al.* (2003), p. 256. © Baywood Publishing Company.

Table 4.7.3 Typical activities of writing partners

- Report progress from previous meeting;
- Discuss any anticipated barriers to writing, and how to overcome them;
- Read and share mutual products; and
- Decide on when next to meet, and on what each partner should bring.

WRITING PARTNERS

The 'Writing Partner' was the name given by Zellermayer *et al.* (1991) to a suite of computer programs designed to help teenagers write essays. Here, I have chosen to use the term to emphasise a slightly different aspect of collaboration – one that emphasises mutual support. Other investigators have used phrases such as 'study buddies', 'personal coaches' or 'mentors' to describe this. Whatever the name, the idea is that one can work together with one, or more, separate partners to facilitate one's writing. The emphasis here is on harnessing the power of social aspects of writing.

Sometimes, partners are allocated, or can be chosen, on writing courses offered by some institutions, and at what are sometimes called 'writers' retreats' (e.g., see Murray and Moore, 2006). Here, it is usually anticipated that there will be an experienced colleague (or mentor) who can assist with the writing of a less-experienced partner. Table 4.7.3 lists the typical activities of writing partners who have joined together. Morss and Murray (2001) and McGrail *et al.* (2006) present evidence to support the effectiveness of writing partners, writing support groups and writing coaches. When working together in these group situations, writers achieved more – more papers were written and published in higher-quality journals, and confidence was boosted.

Formal arrangements are probably helpful, but they are not always necessary. Working informally with different colleagues on a variety of tasks, sharing the writing, responding collectively to the referees, and correcting the proofs together can be mutually satisfying tasks.

REFERENCES

American Psychological Association (2001). *Publication manual of the American Psychological Association* (5th edn). Washington: American Psychological Association.

Abt, H. A. (2007). The frequencies of multinational papers in various sciences. *Scientometrics*, 72(1), 105–15.

Bahr, A. H. & Zemon, M. (2000). Collaborative authorship in the journal literature: Perspectives for academic librarians who wish to publish. *College & Research Libraries*, 61(5), 410–19.

Duque, R. B., Ynalvez, M., Sooryamoorthy, R., Mbatia, P., Dzorgbo, D-B. S. & Schrum, W. (2005). Collaboration paradox. *Social Studies of Science*, 35(5), 755–85.

Hartley, J., Pennebaker, J. W. & Fox, C. (2003). Using new technology to assess the academic writing styles of male and female pairs and individuals. *Journal of Technical Writing and Communication*, 33(3), 243–61.

Lee, S. & Bozeman, B. (2005). The impact of research collaboration on scientific productivity. *Social Studies of Science*, 35(5), 673–702.

Lewison, G. & Hartley, J. (2005). What's in a title? Numbers of words and the presence of colons. *Scientometrics*, 63(2), 341–56.

McGrail, M. R., Rickard, C. M. & Jones, R. (2006). Publish or perish: A systematic review of interventions to increase academic publication rates. *Higher Education Research & Development*, 25(1), 19–25.

Morss, K. & Murray, R. (2001). Researching academic writing within a structured programme: Insights and outcomes. *Studies in Higher Education*, 26(1), 35–52.

Murray, R. & Moore, S. (2006). *The handbook of academic writing: A fresh approach.* Maidenhead: Open University Press.

Sharples, M. (1999). *How we write: Writing as creative design.* London: Routledge.

Wigg, W. D., Dunn, L., Liewehr, D. J., Steinberg, S. M., Thurman, P. W., Barrett, J. C. & Birkinshaw, J. (2006). Scientific collaboration results in higher citation rates of published articles. *Pharmacotherapy*, 26(6), 759–67.

Zellermayer, M., Salomon, G., Globerson, T. & Givon, H. (1991). Enhancing writing related metacognitions through a computerised writing partner. *American Educational Research Journal*, 28(2), 373–91.

FURTHER READING

Speck, B. W., Johnson, T. R., Dice, C. P. & Heaton, L. B. (Eds.). (1999). *Collaborative writing: An annotated bibliography.* Westport, Connecticut: Greenwood Press.

Woods, P. (1999). Collaborative writing. Chapter 6 in *Successful writing for qualitative researchers.* (pp. 97–111). London: Routledge.

Wray, K. B. (2006). Scientific authorship in the age of collaborative research. *Studies in the History and Philosophy of Science*, 37(3), 505–14.

Chapter 4.8

Productive writers

Some people write more than others. Some write a good deal more. What motivates these writers? How do they do it? Do we want to do it too?

There have been several studies of productive writers – but only a few recent ones that discuss writers enmeshed in new technology. The somewhat earlier studies fall into two main, but sometimes overlapping, categories:

1   studies of the faculty in a particular department or institution to see what organisational factors are associated with high productivity; and
2   studies of individuals who score highly on various measures of productivity in particular disciplines.

Most of these papers report data from postal questionnaires, but there are one or two with face-to-face and telephone interviews. Zainab (1999) and Barjak (2005) provide major overviews of the field.

Papers on productive faculties can be found for the following disciplines:

* agricultural education – Kotrlik *et al.* (2002);
* biology, chemistry, mathematics and physics – Allison and Long (1990);
* clinical pharmacy – Jungnickel and Creswell (1994);
* economics – Golden and Carstensen (1992);
* higher education – Creamer and McGuire (1998);
* librarianship – Budd (1995); and
* physical therapy – Holcomb *et al.* (1990).

Papers on productive individuals can be found for the following disciplines:

* ancient history and classical archaeology – Hemlin (1996);
* arts and humanities – Hemlin and Gustafsson (1996);
* biochemistry and cell biology – Fonseca *et al.* (1997);
* education – Tschannen-Moran and Nestor-Baker (2004);
* English – Hemlin (1996);
* information science – Cronin and Meho (2007);

- physical education – Ransdell *et al.* (2001);
- physics – Hermanowicz (2006);
- psychology – Hartley and Branthwaite (1989);
- science – Prpic (1996; 2002); and
- writing – Walters *et al.* (2007).

What do these studies tell us if we think about academic writing in terms of the intrinsic and extrinsic rewards of writing, and the differences between writers discussed in Chapter 1.1?

FACULTY VARIABLES

The research listed above indicates that the following factors are, generally speaking, important here (although there are some national differences: Teodorescu, 2000):

- rank   (professors usually publish more than lecturers);
- prestige of institution   (the higher the prestige of the institution, the higher the production rate);
- time allocated for research   (the more the better);
- time spent on teaching   (the less the better);
- number of graduate students   (need some but not too many);
- number of teaching assistants   (helpful, if they work for you);
- number of colleagues   (some needed, but not too many);
- support from head of the department   (helpful, if not essential); and
- support from university management   (helpful, if not essential).

INDIVIDUAL DIFFERENCES

Productive writers are usually defined in terms of the number of their publications relative to others. Such writers vary a great deal in how they write, but research suggests that the following factors are important:

- gender   (men generally publish more than women, particularly in the sciences – but women are catching up);
- age   (productivity rises relatively quickly to a career maximum in the early forties, and then

gradually declines, but there are individual and disciplinary differences; see Figure 4.8.1); and

- personality
  - − motivation (productive writers are highly motivated);
  - − work habits (productive writers have regular work habits: they write something nearly everyday);
  - − collaboration (productive writers collaborate more, especially in the sciences);
  - − persistence (productive writers keep at it, and revise and resubmit rejected papers);
  - − opportunism (productive writers seize opportunities).

NOBEL LAUREATES

One class of productive authors that has received special attention is the Nobel laureate. Such laureates are usually highly productive in two ways − in the quality of their contributions and in the number of their publications. Table 4.8.1 provides some data in this respect. It shows that, for these laureates, most of them start publishing at an early age, all of them have joint publications, and that most (but not all) have more joint- than single-author papers.

PROBLEMS OF MEASUREMENT

In most of the studies of productive authors listed above, productivity was measured by the number of publications, rather than their quality. For example, in Hartley and Branthwaite's (1989) study − carried out before impact factors and research assessment exercises − the participants' total productivity scores were arrived at by asking them how many items they had published in various categories over three years. These numbers were then multiplied by various weightings: e.g. books were given five marks; book chapters three marks; edited collections of previously published papers two marks; and academic papers one mark. In this study, no differentiation was made between single and joint or multiple authorship, and books were rated as the most important contributions.

Today, it is more common to find that only *journal* publications are counted, and that each contribution is weighted by the number of authors. In some studies, the number of citations for each paper and the journal impact factor are also included (e.g. see Fonseca *et al.*, 1997; Kotrlik *et al.*, 2002), and, because new technology figures highly in productivity, we may well expect future studies of productive authors to assess how they use the Internet to enhance their productivity.

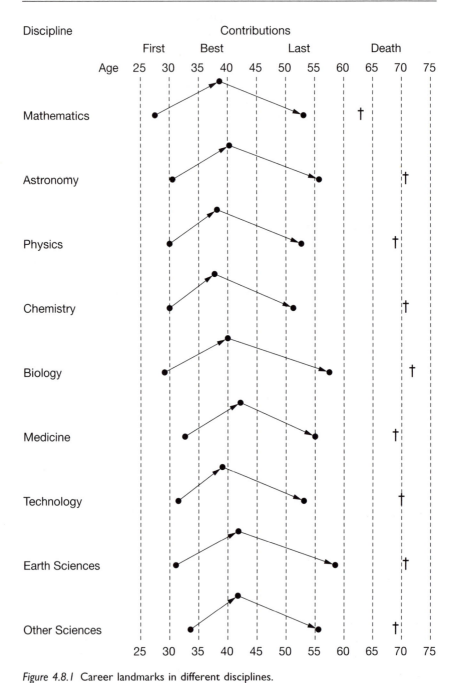

Figure 4.8.1 Career landmarks in different disciplines.

From Simonton (1994), p. 188. Reproduced with permission of the author and Guilford Press.

Table 4.8.1 A portrait of Nobel laureates in terms of age, publication and collaboration

Specialism (period of coverage)	Age at first publication	No. of single author papers	No. of joint publications	Total no. of publications	Highest no. of authors per paper	Age at Nobel award
Physicist C. V. Raman (1906–1970)	18	324	141	465	6	42
Geneticist B. McClintock (1926–1984)	24	66	12	78	4	81
Astrophysicist S. Chandrasekhar (1928–1990)	18	63	317	380	3	73
Crystallographer D. C. Hodgkin (1932–1988)	22	66	144	210	13	54
Physicist P. G. de Gennes (1956–1995)	24	267	155	422	7	59
Chemist[a] J. Heeger (1960–2004)	25	37	709	746	13	41
Physiologist[b] L. H. Hartwell (1961–2001)	22	20	88	108	14	62
Physicist[c] A. J. Leggett (1964–2004)	26	122	72	194	15	59
Femtochemist A. H. Zewail (1976–1994)	30	30	216	246	6	53
Atomic physicist W. Ketterle (1982–2002)	20	18	97	115	14	44
Fullerene chemist H. W. Kroto (1985–2000)	26	20	170	190	16	67

Notes
a   Data from Angadi, M., Koganuramath, M. M., Kademani, B. S., Kumbar, B. D. and Jange, S. (2007). Scientometric portrait of Nobel laureate Alan J. Heeger. Proceedings of the Third International Conference on Webometrics, Informatrics and Scientometrics, New Delhi: India.
b   Data from Angadi, M., Koganuramath, M. M., Kademani, B.S., Kalyane, V. L. and Sen, B. K. (2004). Scientometric portrait of Nobel laureate Leland H. Hartwell. Proceedings of the International Workshop in Webometrics, Informetrics and Scientometrics, Roorkee, India, pp. 10–30. (See Reprints Archives in Library and Information Science: http://eprints.rclis.org/.)
c   Data from Angadi, M., Koganuramath, M. M., Kademani, B. S., Kumbar, B. D. and Jange, S. (2006). Nobel Laureate Anthony J. Leggett: A scientometric portrait. *Annals of Library and Information Studies*, 53(4), 203–12.

Adapted from and with additions to Table 2 in Kademani *et al.* (2005), p. 266 with permission of the authors and the copyright holder, Akademiai Kiado.

NEW TECHNOLOGY AND PRODUCTIVITY

Barjak (2006a; 2006b) has examined the influence of new technology on productivity. In his 2006a paper, Barjak outlined two ways in which new technology can impact on scientific academic writing. He notes that:

1 In general, more information is available over computer networks, and the search for, and retrieval of, information is faster.
2 Access to remote instruments and data sets is easier and faster.

However, he also observes:

1 Learning to use new technology can slow people down.
2 There is a problem with information overload.
3 More productive academics become more visible to their peers, and thus receive more requests for publications, more comments and correspondence.

Barjak (2006a) reported the results obtained from a survey carried out with approximately 1,500 scientists from five academic disciplines (astronomy, chemistry, computer science, economics and psychology) in seven European countries. The participants were asked to describe their use of new technology over a period of two years (2001 to 2002). The results showed quite clearly that the respondents using new technology produced significantly more working papers, journal articles, book chapters, monographs, reports and conference presentations than did the respondents who did not.

In his 2006b paper, Barjak reports that these results were nonlinear, with the very productive scientists using the Internet more, and the much less productive ones using it less, than would be expected according to their productivity. In short, the more productive these scientists were, the more they used new technology.

Such results of course, as Barjak points out, do not necessarily imply a causal factor, and the participants who used multiple methods to communicate did not necessarily achieve higher publication rates than those who used only one method (such as email) a great deal. Furthermore, new technology has replaced a lot of the old technology (email for the telephone and the letter, for example), so that it is inappropriate to say that new technology (in this case, email) has actually changed what academics do. In most cases, new technology allows academics to do what they did before more efficiently. It is when we get to the next generation of new technology that changes in how we write and publish will seem much more radical.

REFERENCES

Allison, P. D. & Long, J. S. (1990). Departmental effects on scientific productivity. *American Sociological Review*, 55(Autumn), 469–78.

Barjak, F. (2005). Research productivity in the Internet era. Series A: Discussion Paper 2005–1. Olten, C.H.4601: Solothurn University of Applied Sciences Northwestern Switzerland.

Barjak, F. (2006a). Research productivity in the Internet era. *Scientometrics*, 68(3), 343–60.

Barjak, F. (2006b). The role of the Internet in informal scholarly communication. *Journal of the American Society for Information Science & Technology*, 57(10), 1350–67.

Budd, J. M. (1995). Faculty publishing productivity: An institutional analysis and comparison with library and other measures. *College & Research Libraries*, 56(6), 547–54.

Creamer, E. G. & McGuire, S. P. (1998). Applying the cumulative advantage perspective to scholarly writers in higher education. *The Review of Higher Education*, 22(1), 73–82.

Cronin, B. & Meho, L. I. (2007). Timelines of creativity: A study of intellectual innovators in information science. *Journal of the American Society for Information Science & Technology*, 58(13), 1948–59.

Fonseca, L., Velloso, S., Wofchuck, S. & De Meis, L. (1997). The importance of human relationships in scientific productivity. *Scientometrics*, 39(2), 159–71.

Golden, J & Carstensen, F. V. (1992). Academic research productivity, department size and organisation: Further results, comment. *Economics of Education Review*, 11(2), 153–60.

Hartley, J. & Branthwaite, A. (1989). The psychologist as wordsmith: A questionnaire study of the writing strategies of productive British psychologists. *Higher Education*, 18, 423–52.

Hemlin, S. (1996). Social studies of the humanities: A case study of research conditions and performance in ancient history and classical archaeology, and English. *Research Evaluation*, April, 53–61.

Hemlin, S. & Gustafsson, M. (1996). Research production in the arts and humanities: A questionnaire study of factors influencing research performance. *Scientometrics*, 37(3), 417–32.

Hermanowicz, J. C. (2006). What does it take to be successful? *Science, Technology & Human Values*, 31(2), 135–52.

Holcolm, J. D., Selker, S. G. & Roush, R. E. (1990). Scholarly productivity: A regional study of physical therapy faculty in schools of allied health. *Physical Therapy*, 70(2), 118–24.

Kademani, B.S., Kalyane, V. L., Kumar, V. & Mohan, L (2005). Nobel laureates: Their publication productivity, collaboration and authorship status. *Scientometrics*, 62(2), 261–8.

Kotrlik, J. W., Bartlett, J. E., Higgins, C. C. & Williams, H. A. (2002). Factors associated with research productivity of agricultural education faculty. *Journal of Agricultural Education*, 43(2), 1–10.

Jungnickel, P. W. & Creswell, J. W. (1994). Workplace correlates and scholarly performance of clinical pharmacy faculty. *Research in Higher Education*, 35(2), 167–94.

Prpic, K. (1996). Scientific fields and eminent scientists productivity patterns and factors. *Scientometrics*, 37(3), 445–71.

Prpic, K. (2002). Gender and productivity differentials in science. *Scientometrics*, 55(1), 27–58.

Randsdell, L. B., Dinger, M. K., Cooke, C. & Beske, S. (2001). Factors related to publication productivity in a sample of female health educators. *American Journal of Health Behavior*, 25(5), 469–80.

Simonton, D. K. (1994). *Greatness: Who makes history and why.* New York: Guilford Press.

Teodorescu, D. (2000). Correlates of faculty production: A cross-national analysis. *Higher Education*, 39(2), 201–22.

Tschannen-Moran, T. & Nestor-Baker, N. (2004). The tacit knowledge of productive scholars in education. *Teachers College Record*, 106(7), 1484–511.

Walters, M., Hunter, S. & Giddens, E. (2007). Qualitative research on what leads to success in professional writing. Retrieved 20 August 2007 from *European Journal for the Scholarship of Teaching & Learning*, 1(2), July (page numbers unspecified) (www.georgiasouthern.edu/ijsotl).

Zainab, A. N. (1999). Personal, academic and departmental correlates of research productivity: A review of the literature. *Malaysian Journal of Library & Information Science*, 4(2), 73–110.

FURTHER READING

Fox, M. F. (2005). Gender, family characteristics, and publication productivity among scientists. *Social Studies of Science*, 35(1), 131–50.

Garfield, E. & Welljams-Dorof (1992). Of Nobel class: A citation perspective on high impact research authors. *Theoretical Medicine*, 13(2), 117–35.

Simonton, D. K. (2007). Creative life cycles in literature: Poets versus novelists, or conceptualists versus experimentalists? *Psychology of Aesthetics, Creativity, and the Arts*, 1(3), 133–9.

Zuckerman, H. (1977). *Scientific elite: Nobel laureates in the United States.* New York: Free Press.

Appendix I

Guidelines for academic writing

Revised list from Hartley, J. (1997). Writing the thesis. In N. Graves & V. Varma (Eds.), *Working for a doctorate* (pp. 97–100). London: Routledge.

1   *Keep in mind your readers – they may not be experts*
    Imagine that you are writing for a fellow colleague – or for one of your students – who is familiar with the conventions of your discipline, but who does not know your area. Readers need to be able to grasp what you did and what you found, and to follow your arguments easily.

2   *Use the first rather than the third person*
    Compare: 'We suggest that . . .' *with* 'This paper suggests that . . .'

3   *Use short, simple words*
    It is easier to understand short, familiar words than technical terms that mean the same thing. *Compare*: 'We assume, from the start . . .' *with* 'We assume, a priori . . .'

4   *Use active tenses*
    It is easier to understand text when writers use active tenses rather than passive ones. *Compare*: 'We found that the chemists varied more than the engineers on a measure of extraversion . . .' *with* 'Greater variation was found on a measure of extraversion with the chemists than with the engineers . . .'

5   *Sequencing in sentences*
    It is more helpful for the reader in English if the subject of the verb comes *before*, and the object *after*, the verb. *Compare*: 'Students need accessible information to become intelligent customers . . .' *with* 'To become intelligent customers, students need accessible information . . .'

6   *Place sequences in order*
    Similarly, it is best to describe procedures in the order that they take place. For example, *compare*: 'Before the experiment commenced, we first briefed the participants on the necessary procedures and any precautions

that they should take . . .' *with* 'We briefed the participants on the necessary procedures and any precautions that they should take before the experiment began . . .'

7   *Avoid negatives*
Negatives, especially double or treble ones, can be confusing. *Compare*: 'The figures provide no indication that the costs would not have been lower if competition had not been restricted . . .' *with* 'The figures provide no indication that competition would have produced higher costs . . .'. Negative qualifications can be used, however, for particular emphasis, and for correcting misconceptions.

8   *Avoid abbreviations*
Many writers use abbreviations for technical terms: for example RAE for research assessment exercise. Too many abbreviations on a page are off-putting. Furthermore, if the abbreviations are unfamiliar to the reader, it is easy for them to forget what they stand for.

9   *Avoid overloading the text with references*
It is difficult to read sentences that end with long lists of supporting references. It is better to cite only the more recent papers that between them summarise earlier research. *Compare*: 'Common practice has been to assume the condition of local equilibrium (for example, see Bickle and others, 1997, and Brady, 2001, for surveys of this research) . . .' *with* 'Common practice has been to assume the condition of local equilibrium (Baumgartner and Rumble, 1988; Bickle and Baker, 1990; Bickle and others, 1995, 1997; Brady, 2001, Cartwright and Valley, 1991; Ferry, 1986, 1994) . . .'

10   *Vary sentence lengths*
It is easier to understand short sentences than it is to understand long ones, because long sentences overload the memory system. Short sentences do not. However, it is good practice to vary sentence lengths, as long strings of short sentences feel 'choppy'.
   As a rule of thumb, I suggest that sentences less than twenty words long are probably fine. Sentences twenty to thirty words long are probably satisfactory. Sentences thirty to forty words long are suspect. Sentences with over forty words in them will probably benefit from re-writing.

11   *Use short paragraphs*
Short paragraphs are easier to read than long ones. Any typescript that has a page of text without at least one new paragraph needs attention!

12   *Use numbers or bullets*
Numbers or 'bullets' are useful if you want to make a series of points within a paragraph. *Compare*: 'Four devices to help the reader of a thesis are a detailed contents page, skeleton outlines for each chapter, headings in the text, and a concluding summary . . .' *with*:

'Four devices to help the reader of a thesis are:

- a detailed contents page
- skeleton outlines for each chapter
- headings in the text
- a concluding summary.'

13 *Settings for lists*

It helps the reader if you use space to list the points in a structurally similar way, for example:

Bullet points for items without any particular order	Numbers for steps in a sequence	Letters for mutually exclusive items
• ———	1 ———	(a) ———
• ———	2 ———	(b) ———
• ———	3 ———	(c) ———

It is best to use *bullets* when each point is of equal value, *numbers* when there is an order, or sequence in the points made, and *letters* for mutually exclusive items.

14 *Use subheadings*

Subheadings label sections so that writers and readers know where they are, and where they are going. Subheadings help the reader to scan, select and retrieve material, as well as to recall it. Subheadings can be written in the form of statements or in the form of questions. If the subheadings are in the form of questions, then the text below must answer them. This helps the author to present – and the reader to follow – the argument.

15 *Print out and revise/edit draft copies*

Print out draft copies when the text is nearing completion. Copies allow you to check more easily the tiny details – punctuation, references, etc. – as well as to get a better feel for the document as a whole. Think about *global* revisions – re-sequencing major portions – and *local* revisions – making changes to individual words and sentences (see Appendix 2).

16 *When in difficulty . . .*

If it is difficult to explain something, think of how you would explain it to a particular person. Think of what you would say, try saying it and then write this down. Then polish it.

17 *Read the text out aloud*

Reading the text out aloud (or silently) to oneself is a useful way of seeing how well the text flows. You may find that you need to insert commas to make text groupings clearer, you may get out of breath because sentences are too long, and you might inadvertently read out a simpler version of the written text. If you do this, change the text to this simpler version.

18 *Ask other people to read your drafts*

Colleagues and students may be willing to read and comment on drafts. Ask them to point out those sentences or sections that they think other readers might find it difficult to follow. People are more willing to point out difficulties for others than they are to admit to their own.

You might to like to do this separately for your tables, graphs and abstracts. Ask your readers to tell you what each of these features says to them.

19 *Read and listen to other authors*

Absorb techniques from other writers you admire. Writers of weekly/monthly columns in magazines, or of weekly talks on radio, often produce pure gems.

20 *Revise continuously . . .*

Never regard the last version of the text as the final one. Put this version on one side and then come back to it a day or two later. Seeing the text with fresh eyes somehow suggests further changes, but draw the line eventually!

Guidelines for revising text

Revised list from Hartley, J. (1997). Writing the thesis. In N. Graves & V. Varma (Eds.), *Working for a doctorate* (p. 103). London: Routledge.

1   Read through the text asking yourself:
    *   Who is the text for?

2   Read through the text again, but this time ask yourself:
    *   What changes do I need to make to help the reader?
    *   How can I make the text easier to follow?

3   To make these changes you may need:
    *   to make big or *global* changes (e.g. rewrite sections); or
    *   to make small or minor *text* changes (e.g. change the original text slightly).

    You will need to decide whether you are going to focus first on global changes or first on text changes.

4   *Global changes* you might like to consider are:
    *   re-sequencing parts of the text
    *   rewriting sections in simpler prose
    *   adding examples
    *   changing examples for better ones
    *   deleting parts that seem confusing.

5   *Text changes* you might like to consider are:
    *   using simpler wording
    *   using shorter sentences
    *   using shorter paragraphs
    *   using active rather than passive tenses
    *   substituting positives for negatives
    *   writing sequences in order
    *   spacing numbered sequences or lists down the page (as here).

6   Keep reading through the revised text from start to finish to see if you want to make any more global changes.

7   Repeat this whole procedure on the revised text some time after making your initial revisions (say twenty-four hours), and do this without looking back at the original text.

8   Repeat stage 7 several times, but draw the line eventually!

Appendix 3

Abbreviations for American states used in citing references

(Source: *Publication Manual of the American Psychological Association* (5th edn) (pp. 217–18) (2001). Washington: American Psychological Association. Reprinted with permission.)

The following cities are used in citing places of publication without their states because they are well known in their own right:

Amsterdam	London	Paris	Tokyo
Baltimore	Los Angeles	Philadelphia	Vienna
Boston	Milan	Rome	
Chicago	Moscow	San Francisco	
Jerusalem	New York	Stockholm	

Abbreviations for states and territories in the USA:

Location	Abbreviation	Location	Abbreviation
Alabama	AL	Missouri	MO
Alaska	AK	Montana	MT
American Samoa	AS	Nebraska	NE
Arizona	AZ	Nevada	NV
Arkansas	AR	New Hampshire	NH
California	CA	New Jersey	NJ
Canal Zone	CZ	New Mexico	NM
Colorado	CO	New York	NY
Connecticut	CT	North Carolina	NC
Delaware	DE	North Dakota	ND
District of		Ohio	OH
Columbia	DC	Oklahoma	OK
Florida	FL	Oregon	OR
Georgia	GA	Pennsylvania	PA
Guam	GU	Puerto Rico	PR
Hawaii	HI	Rhode Island	RI

Idaho	ID	South Carolina	SC
Illinois	IL	South Dakota	SD
Indiana	IN	Tennessee	TN
Iowa	IA	Texas	TX
Kansas	KS	Utah	UT
Kentucky	KY	Vermont	VT
Louisiana	LA	Virginia	VA
Maine	ME	Virgin Islands	VI
Maryland	MD	Washington	WA
Massachusetts	MA	West Virginia	WV
Michigan	MI	Wisconsin	WI
Minnesota	MN	Wyoming	WY
Mississippi	MS		

Author index

Subject index